VINCENZO VENEZIA

healing your inner child

Reclaiming your Little Child That is Wounded Within You, Overcome Trauma and Let Go of the Past to Find Peace

Contents

INTRODUCTION

Do you remember being 12? The energy you had, how happy you were, the confidence you had, those curious eyes, and that mischievous little mind. Oh, how simple life was at the time! No bills, no responsibilities, no anxiety—just "hakuna matata" on the daily agenda. The greatest amount of anxiety we had was brought on by Mom being upset, not how to survive the next few days with a 3-digit PIN as a bank balance.

Life hit us in the face, and somewhere along the way, we all grew up, and our priorities changed. Instead of putting on a smile the entire day, we are all wearing blank faces. In the race of life, we forget to enjoy the little moments, the fun, lighthearted side of life. We got so entangled in "creating a future" that we buried the kid within us so deeply that it would never surface again.

You know, it's funny how we humans have this innate need to please others. We're constantly trying to make sure everyone around us is happy, often at the expense of our own happiness. And a big part of that is because we're scared that if we don't keep everyone happy, we'll lose their love and affection. But in the process of trying to please everyone else, we often neglect that little inner child within us.

And it's not just a psychological thing; there's a neurobiological aspect to it, too. Certain changes in the brain, like in the prefrontal cortex, can lead to more advanced thinking, which can make us better at regulating our emotions and impulses. But as we become more sophisticated and adult-like in our thinking, we may start to rely less on raw emotions, which is what our inner child is often in touch with. So, in a way, we're kind of pushing away that childlike part of ourselves as we try to become more mature.

You know when something happens, and you suddenly feel like a kid again? Like, maybe a coworker says something snarky, and you're suddenly seven years old and in tears? Yeah, that's your inner child. It's that part of you that holds all your childhood memories, both the good and the bad. And sometimes, those bad memories can come back to haunt us. But don't worry; there's a way to deal with it. It's called "reparenting" your inner child. It's about looking back at your past experiences and understanding why you feel a certain way now. It's not about changing who you are; it's about healing the wounds from your past so you can move forward in a positive direction.

"The concept of the Child Within has been a part of our world culture for at least two thousand years. Carl Jung called it the "Divine Child", and Emmet Fox called it the "Wonder Child." Psychotherapists Alice Miller and Donald Winnicott refer to it as the "true self." Many in the field of alcoholism and other chemical dependence call it the "inner child."

— Charles Whitfield

Everyone has an "inner child" that represents their early years, the different developmental stages they have experienced, or the playful and youthful dreams they had. Connecting with this inner child can bring back memories of carefree times and help us cope with difficult situations.

In the words of the late great Walt Disney,

"Adults are only kids grown up, anyway."

Some people find that reconnecting with their inner child helps them feel more grounded, authentic, and in touch with their emotions. It can also be a helpful way to heal from past traumas or difficulties that may have affected you during your childhood.

Not everyone has positive associations with childhood, and their inner child may be a vulnerable, neglected, or traumatized part of themselves that they have tried to hide to protect themselves.

As adults, we tend to trap our inner child and prevent ourselves from fully embracing our natural sense of curiosity, playfulness, and authenticity to avoid dealing with tough or painful emotions. We suffocate the child inside us by being excessively risk-averse, refusing to attempt new things or venture outside our comfort zone, clinging to the past, and refusing to move forward. This can involve dwelling on past traumas or mistakes or simply holding on to old thinking patterns that no longer serve us. Another way we do this is by being overly critical of ourselves and striving for perfection.

"When our inner child is not nurtured and nourished, our minds gradually close to new ideas, unprofitable commitments, and the surprises of the spirit."

- Brennan Manning.

Rekindling your inner child can bring a sense of playfulness and creativity back into your life, help you feel more connected to your true self and unique interests and passions, and help you rediscover your sense of wonder and curiosity. It can also help you tap into and process any unresolved emotions or traumas from your childhood, leading to improved emotional well-being and a greater sense of inner peace. By embracing your inner child, you can feel more spontaneous, carefree, and present in the moment, able to enjoy life fully.

Additionally, the concept of the inner child has been incorporated into various forms of therapy, such as inner child work and play therapy, to help individuals process and heal from past traumas and challenges. These therapies often involve activities that allow individuals to tap into their inner child and explore their emotions in a safe and supportive environment.

Reconnecting with your inner child means taking the time to connect with and understand your emotional and psychological self as it was when you were a child. This can involve exploring childhood memories, thoughts, and feelings and trying to understand how they have shaped you as an adult. It can also require tapping into the sense of wonder, playfulness, and creativity you may have had as a child and incorporating those qualities into your adult life.

There are many ways to reconnect with your inner child. Some people find it helpful to engage in activities they enjoyed as a child, such as playing sports, creating art, or playing music. Others find it helpful to journal their childhood experiences or talk to a therapist about their memories and feelings. Some people find it helpful to spend time in nature, which can be a soothing and nourishing environment that can help you feel more connected to your inner self.

Recovering the mini-you can also be helpful in practicing mindfulness, which involves bringing your attention to the present moment and observing your thoughts and feelings without judgment. This can help you better understand the thoughts and feelings that may be driving your behavior.

"Three things are striking about inner child work: the speed with which people change when they do this work; the depth of that change; and the power and creativity that result when wounds from the past are healed."

- John Bradshaw

Ultimately, the most important thing is to find what works best for you and to be patient with yourself. It may take time to re-connect with your inner child, but with practice and self-compassion, you can develop a deeper understanding of yourself and your needs.

Let's not forget to have some fun and let loose every once in a while! Being in touch with your inner child means not taking everything too seriously; it's about giving yourself permission to play, discover, chuckle, and appreciate the world with wonder and excitement.

"We must remain as close to the flowers, the grass, and the butterflies as the child is who is not yet so much taller than they are."

- Friedrich Nietzsche.

Suppressing pain does not resolve it, and it can often resurface in adulthood through issues in personal relationships or difficulty in meeting one's own needs. Embracing your inner child can be a rewarding and healing process. It's important to be kind and compassionate toward yourself as you navigate this process. Healing the inner child can be a process that takes time. This book will get you started on this illuminating journey of self-healing.

PART 1 - WHAT DOES RECONNECTING WITH YOUR INNER CHILD MEAN?

CHAPTER 1: WHAT DOES RECONNECTING WITH YOUR INNER CHILD MEAN?

As human beings, we are not born with all the knowledge and skills necessary to navigate the world around us. Instead, we must learn and grow as we age. Children are particularly adept at this process, as they learn through both experience and play. However, as adults, we can also continue to learn and grow to thrive in a rapidly changing world. One way to do this is to reconnect with our inner child, as the childlike mindset of openness and curiosity can be incredibly effective in facilitating learning.

It is important to note that not everyone's life experiences are perfect. For some individuals, reconnecting with the childlike learner may also require facing difficult emotions and memories. This is where inner child work comes in, as it can aid in addressing and healing past traumas to move forward with open learning and adaptation. Inner child work can help us overcome obstacles that may have been learned in childhood and allow us to continue growing and learning in a positive and fulfilling way. Rekindling and embracing the mini-you can be a rich and rewarding experience that can bring more joy, creativity, and connection into your life.

Yes, all of that sounds great, but what does "reconnecting with your inner child" even mean?

Yoga teachers and meditation experts keep going on about "getting in touch with the child inside." And I am certainly not expecting, so who is this inner child?

What Is Meant by Our "Inner Child?"

Think back to when you were a little kid in the first grade. You're playing with your classmates on the playground, running around, laughing, and having fun. You decide to get on the swings and show the others how high you can jump off them. You proudly swing yourself and get ready to take off mid-swing to showcase your magnificent jump. But then, you trip and fall to the ground face-down. You look up to see all the other kids start laughing at you and pointing at the mud on your face and your clothes.

You might not remember exactly what happened or who was there, but you can still feel the embarrassment and shame. You can still see the tears in your eyes and feel the pain in your head and knees. And you might even remember telling yourself, "I'll never put myself in that situation again."

Even though the bump on your head healed, the memory of that day still haunts you. You're not in control of it. Years later, that little 5-year-old version of yourself is still running the show. It's hard for you to take risks because you're still scared of being laughed at, even though you don't remember the incident. Now, even if you are confident that you can do something, you cannot do it because you can still hear those kids laughing and pointing at you. So, you let the fear of failure take hold of you while you hide in the shadow of your mistakes.

When we start working on healing our inner child, we're opening up to a more vulnerable and sensitive part of ourselves. We can be both the adult and the child simultaneously, giving ourselves unconditional love, understanding, and support.

What Is the Inner Child?

The "inner child" is a psychological concept that refers to the childlike aspect of a person's psyche, representing their emotional and personal growth. It is believed to hold the feelings, thoughts, and memories of a person's childhood and influence adult behaviors and attitudes.

The inner child is often seen as a way to access and understand the emotional self, and it can be a helpful tool for personal growth and healing. Some people believe that the inner child is a source of creativity, playfulness, and spontaneity and that reconnecting with this aspect of the self can be enriching and nourishing.

When we work on our inner child, we're basically giving ourselves the parenting we didn't get. We realize how all those past experiences shape how we act and react as adults. It's about taking a good hard look at the parts of ourselves that we've ignored or forgotten about and then reconnecting with them. It helps us understand why we do the things we do. It's about discovering what makes us tick, what sets us off, and what we really want in life.

Healing and understanding our childhood experiences through inner child work helps us to recognize how those experiences shape our adult behaviors and reactions. This process involves evaluating and addressing the neglected aspects of ourselves from childhood and reconnecting with the childlike parts of ourselves.

When you work with a therapist, they might not refer to it specifically as "inner child work." They might call it "healing the child within" or "embracing your child archetype" instead. It could also be a part of "shadow work," which is about exploring and understanding the hidden parts of ourselves. As children, we often learn to push down emotions like sadness and anger, which become our shadows. Inner child work helps to bring those repressed feelings to light and heal them.

Working on your inner child is an important aspect of self-discovery and personal growth. Your inner child is the part of you that holds all of your childhood memories, feelings, and emotions. It's the part of you that still feels like a child, even though you may be an adult now.

The idea of an inner child comes from the work of psychiatrist Carl Jung. It refers to the part of us that still holds on to the emotions, thoughts, and experiences of our childhood. This includes both the positive aspects, such as innocence, wonder, and creativity, as well as the negative aspects, such as past traumas or unresolved emotions. Inner child work involves becoming aware of and addressing these past experiences in order to heal and move forward in a positive direction.

Inner Child Work is all about understanding that we still have younger parts of ourselves inside us, even as adults. These parts may have different experiences and needs and can come out when we're feeling triggered or upset. Sometimes, we might not even realize that a younger part of us is causing our reactions.

But by recognizing and addressing these parts, we can start to heal past traumas and respond to our wounds in a healthier way.

The Child Archetype by Carl Jung

The "child archetype" is a concept developed by Carl Jung, a Swiss psychiatrist and psychoanalyst. Jung believed that there were certain universal patterns or themes that existed in the human psyche, which he called archetypes.

The child archetype represents the innate sense of wonder and innocence that exists within each person. It is associated with creativity, spontaneity, and playfulness. The child archetype can also represent the potential for growth and development.

In terms of psychology, the child archetype can manifest in different ways in a person's life. For example, a person who is in touch with their child archetype may be more open to new experiences and more willing to take risks. On the other hand, a person who has repressed their child archetype may be more closed off and resistant to change.

In terms of mythology and storytelling, the child archetype often appears as the "hero's journey," where the hero (child) goes on a journey to gain knowledge and power to become a full-fledged adult.

It's important to note that the child archetype is not just limited to children; it exists in every person and can manifest at any stage of life. By embracing and understanding the child archetype, one can tap into their innate sense of wonder and creativity, leading to personal growth and fulfillment.

"The "child" is all that is abandoned and exposed and at the same time divinely powerful; the insignificantly dubious beginning and the triumphal end. The "eternal child" in man is an indescribable experience, an incongruity, a handicap, and a divine prerogative; an imponderable that determines the ultimate worth or worthlessness of a personality."

— C. G. Jung

Jung believed that this archetype was present in all humans and could be a source of creativity and renewal. Each person has a unique combination of archetypes that make up their personality, and these archetypes can change and evolve throughout a person's life.

In terms of therapy, Jung believed that by becoming aware of and working with one's archetypes, a person could gain a deeper understanding of themselves and their motivations, leading to personal growth and healing.

It's also worth noting that the child archetype can manifest in both positive and negative ways. An unhealthy expression of the child archetype could be seen in a person who is overly dependent, easily manipulated, irresponsible, or refuses to grow up and take responsibility. On the other hand, a healthy expression of the child archetype can be seen in a person who maintains a sense of wonder, curiosity, and playfulness while also taking on responsibilities and being an adult.

The child archetype is a complex and multi-faceted concept but understanding it can provide insight into one's own personality and behavior and can lead to personal growth and healing.

Types Of Child Archetypes

Carl Jung identified 12 types of archetypes, including the child archetype, which can manifest in different forms. Here is a brief description of each of these child archetypes:

1. **The Wounded Child** is a child archetype that has experienced some form of trauma or abuse. They are stuck in a cycle of pity and blame. They may feel helpless, vulnerable, and in need of protection.

2. **The Orphaned Child** is a child archetype that feels abandoned or disconnected from others. They might often push others away or have accumulated trust issues. They may feel a sense of loss or a desire to belong.

3. **The Magical Child** is a child archetype full of wonder and awe. They are courageous and may act against the current. They may have a vivid imagination and a sense of playfulness.

4. **The Nature Child** is a child archetype that feels a deep connection to nature. They may be in tune with the environment and have a strong sense of ecology. They are often sensitive yet not afraid to tackle obstacles.

5. **The Divine Child** is a child archetype that embodies purity and innocence. They may have a strong sense of spirituality and a connection to a higher power. They are naturally loving, caring, kind, and empathetic.

6. **The Eternal Child** is a child archetype that retains a sense of youthfulness and playfulness throughout their life. They may have childlike wonder and curiosity. They are afraid to grow up, stuck in an earlier stage of life.

7. **The Hero Child** is a child archetype driven by a sense

of purpose and a desire to do good. They may have a strong sense of morality and justice.

8. **The Needy Child** is a child archetype that relies on others for support and guidance. They may struggle with feelings of inadequacy and dependence. They try to fill the void within them with the help of things or people.

9. **The Trickster Child** is a child archetype that delights in mischief and play. They may be clever and mischievous. They know how to entertain others and carry a good sense of humor.

10. **The Fairy Tale Child** is a child archetype that embodies the archetypal hero of traditional fairy tales. They may have a sense of adventure and a desire to seek new experiences. They tend to be overly optimistic and fear being punished.

11. **The Caregiver** is a child archetype, also known as the nurturer or the helper. They have a strong urge to protect and help the people around them. They love and care unconditionally and often end up overstepping boundaries.

12. **The Lover** is a child archetype that is the team-builder, the friend, and the intimate one. They

carry a deep fear of rejection and can be easily suppressed. They lack self-love and have issues with attachment or addiction.

The Wounded Child Archetype

The archetype of the wounded child represents a psychological pattern or theme that emerges in the human psyche, often due to early childhood experiences that have been traumatic or damaging in some way. This archetype can take on many forms, but it generally involves a sense of deep emotional pain, vulnerability, and woundedness that can manifest in various behaviors and relationships throughout one's life.

When someone identifies with the Wounded Child archetype more strongly than any other child archetype, it indicates that their painful and abusive childhood experiences have significantly impacted their adult life. This can be difficult to navigate and may lead to negative consequences, such as difficulties in forming healthy relationships or achieving career goals.

Those who identify with the Wounded Child archetype may blame it for their struggles and view the world through a negative lens. They may be more prone to cynicism and pessimism, making it harder for them to see the positive aspects of life.

The wounds created by their childhood experiences can color how they experience the rest of their life, leaving them more vulnerable to further trauma and wounding. This can create a vicious cycle of pain and hurt as the individual continues to re-experience their past wounds in their present life.

1. Do you often feel like you missed out on a nurturing, stable, or secure childhood?

2. Do you struggle to trust others or form close relationships due to fear of being hurt or betrayed?

3. Do you struggle with feelings of abandonment, neglect, or rejection?

4. Do you struggle with feelings of shame, inadequacy, or self-blame?

5. Do you struggle to assert yourself or pursue your goals due to fear of failure or rejection?

If you answered "yes" to any of these questions, you might identify with the wounded child archetype. However, it's important to keep in mind that this is a complex psychological pattern that requires a thorough evaluation by a qualified mental health professional to understand and address it fully.

Types Of Wounded Child Archetype

The concept of wounded child archetypes is often used in psychological and spiritual work to describe deep-seated emotional wounds that people may carry from childhood. Here are twelve common wounded child archetypes:

1. **The Failure Child** archetype is someone who feels like they can never do anything right and is constantly falling short of expectations. They may feel like they are always disappointing others and struggle with low self-esteem.

2. **The Unsafe Child** archetype is someone who feels like the world is a dangerous place where they cannot trust anyone to keep them safe. This may result in feelings of anxiety and hypervigilance as they try to protect themselves from perceived threats.

3. **The Insufficient Child** archetype is someone who feels like they are never enough and always needs to do more to be worthy of love. This can lead to feelings of inadequacy and a constant need to prove themselves to others.

4. **The Deprived Child** archetype is someone who feels like they are missing something essential and can never quite fill the void. They may feel a sense of emptiness

or longing that they cannot satisfy.

5. **The Invisible Child** archetype is someone who feels like they don't matter and that their needs and wants are unimportant. They may struggle to assert themselves and may feel invisible or ignored by others.

6. **The Freak Child** archetype is someone who feels like they are different or strange, making them unlovable. They may feel like they don't fit in and may struggle to find acceptance from others.

7. **The Burden Child** archetype is someone who feels like they are a burden to others and are constantly inconveniencing those around them. They may struggle to ask for help or support and feel guilty about needing assistance.

8. **The Abandoned Child** archetype is someone who feels like they have been left alone and that no one is coming back for them. They may struggle with trust and feel like they cannot rely on others to be there.

9. **The Too Much Child** archetype is someone who feels like they are too intense or overwhelming for others and need to tone themselves down to be accepted. They may struggle with expressing themselves authentically and feel like they need to hide parts of them-

selves.

10. **The Disposable Child** archetype is someone who feels like they are easily replaceable and that their presence doesn't make a significant impact on anyone's life. They may struggle with feelings of worthlessness and feel like they don't matter to others.

11. **The Mistake Child** archetype is someone who feels like they are inherently flawed and that their existence is a mistake. They may struggle with feelings of shame and self-doubt.

12. **The Betrayed Child** archetype is someone who feels like someone they trusted has betrayed them and that they cannot trust anyone anymore. They may struggle with forming close relationships and feel like they need to protect themselves from being hurt again.

Exploring these wounded child archetypes can help individuals gain insight into their emotional wounds and develop greater self-awareness. This, in turn, can facilitate the process of healing and growth.

Now that you know the 12 archetypes of the wounded inner child, you may be wondering which one applies to you. Here is a simple test you can take to identify your archetype:

Take a moment to reflect on your childhood and any negative experiences you may have had. Consider how these experiences have affected your thoughts, emotions, and behaviors in adulthood.

Read through the descriptions of the 12 archetypes above and see which one resonates with you the most. You may find that you identify with more than one or that none quite fit.

Take some time to journal about your chosen archetype and how it has affected your life. Reflect on how your wounds have influenced your behaviors, relationships, and sense of self, and consider what steps you can take to start healing.

Identifying your wounded inner child archetype is just the first step in the healing process. It takes time, patience, and self-compassion to work through the emotional and psychological damage of childhood trauma.

Studies Based on the Phenomenon of the "Child Archetype"

Some researchers have applied the concept of archetypes to the study of literature, film, and other forms of popular culture and have found that the child archetype is a common theme in many stories and myths.

Others have used the concept of archetypes in clinical settings, using techniques such as active imagination and dream analysis to help patients access and work with their archetypes to promote personal growth and healing.

"Regression in the Countertransference: Working with the Archetype of the Abandoned Child" is a that explores the concept of the child archetype in the context of psychoanalytic therapy. The study was published in the International Journal of Psychoanalytic Self-Psychology in 2009.

The study examines the phenomenon of "regression in the countertransference," which refers to the tendency of therapists to respond unconsciously to their patients in a way that reflects their own unresolved emotional issues. The study's author suggests that the archetype of the abandoned child, which represents feelings of abandonment, rejection, and longing, is particularly relevant in this context. It also highlights the importance of therapist self-awareness and understanding of archetypes in the therapy process, particularly when working with patients who have experienced abandonment or rejection.

"The Care of Regressed Patients and the Child Archetype" is a that explores the concept of the child archetype in the context of psychoanalytic therapy. The study was published in the Journal of Analytical Psychology in 1964. It examines the phenomenon of "regression" in patients, which refers to the tendency of individuals to revert to earlier, less mature stages of development in response to stress or emotional trauma. Working with the child archetype in therapy can benefit the patients, as it can help them reconnect with their inner child and express and integrate repressed emotions and memories.

The study argues that the child archetype is particularly relevant in the care of regressed patients, as it represents feelings of vulnerability, dependence, and longing for nurturing.

Reconnecting with your inner child means embracing these childlike qualities and allowing yourself to take life less seriously. It can involve engaging in activities that bring you joy and allow you to tap into your creativity, such as playing, creating art, or engaging in hobbies.

Embracing fun, spontaneity, and a sense of awe and wonder can also involve letting go of the need to conform to the expectations of others or to be "perfect." It means ignoring critics and the urge to take life too seriously and instead focusing on what feels right and authentic for you.

For example, you might reconnect with your inner child by taking a dance class, building a fort, or creating a piece of art just for fun. You might also practice letting go of judgment or self-consciousness and simply allowing yourself to enjoy the present moment.

Who Should Opt for Inner Child Work

Inner-child work is a therapeutic approach that can be beneficial for anyone who has experienced trauma or negative experiences in their past, whether it be explicit traumas such as physical and sexual abuse or more subtle forms of neglect and abuse such as emotional misattunement or dismissal of feelings, opinions, and needs.

For those who have experienced explicit traumas, inner child work can provide a safe space for individuals to process and understand the emotions and memories associated with these traumas, which can be very powerful for healing. For those who experienced more subtle forms of neglect and abuse, inner-child work can help to understand how these experiences may have shaped their thoughts, feelings, and behaviors in adulthood and how to address these issues.

Even if you had a good enough upbringing, inner-child work could be beneficial, as everyone experiences hurt and trauma at some point in life. Inner-child work can also be helpful for individuals who experience emotional pain due to societal pressure to be constantly busy and working, with little time for rest, play, and connection.

Inner-child work can help to address these issues by providing a safe space for individuals to process and understand their emotions and experiences and to develop a more nurturing and supportive inner parent that can guide and support the inner child.

"Inner child work helps us get to the root of the problem - the core wounding - instead of putting a Band-Aid over the pain and hoping it gets better."

-Robert Jackman

Healing your inner child can have a big impact on a lot of different areas of your life. Maybe you've struggled with anxiety or had a hard time setting boundaries in relationships.

For example, let's say you've always had trouble saying "no" to people. You might find yourself constantly going along with things even if you don't want to, or you might feel guilty when you do put your foot down.

This could be rooted in your childhood. Maybe your parents were always demanding, and you never felt like you could express your own needs. Or maybe they were always permissive, and you never learned to set boundaries.

By exploring your past and "reparenting" your inner child, you can start to understand where this tendency comes from. And once you understand it, you can start to make changes and set healthier boundaries for yourself.

Overall, inner-child work can be beneficial for anyone, as it can help individuals heal from past traumas and negative experiences and understand how these experiences have shaped their thoughts, feelings, and behaviors in adulthood. It can also help individuals develop a more nurturing and supportive inner parent, leading to improved emotional regulation, self-awareness, and self-worth.

CHAPTER 2: WHAT DOES IT FEEL LIKE TO HAVE A WOUNDED INNER CHILD?

"Your life is precious. You've only got one. Don't waste it on bad relationships, on bad marriages, on bad jobs, on bad people. Waste it wisely on what you want to do."

- Eric Idle

Do you feel a sense of fear, stress, anxiety, panic, dread, or perfectionism, or find yourself avoiding certain situations, people, or places? These are all signs that your inner child is wounded and seeking safety.

When the inner child is in charge, it makes decisions and governs behavior based on unconscious beliefs and memories from the past that it perceives as safe.

It's important to understand that the inner child may not fully understand the current reality and may not be aware of the changes that have occurred.

Our daily experiences and challenges may hold clues to deeper, unconscious wounds from our past. By being mindful of our emotional responses and exploring the psychological bruises we carry, we can gain insight into the sources of our pain and work towards healing and growth.

Some individuals may become "people-pleasers," constantly putting the needs and wants of others before their own. This may be due to a childhood in which they were taught to prioritize the needs of others and to suppress their own emotions, interests, and desires. As a result, they may struggle to assert themselves and feel a constant sense of guilt or shame if they don't fulfill the expectations of others.

On the other hand, other individuals may become highly narcissistic, viewing others as objects to be used for their own gain. This can be the result of a childhood in which they were taught to prioritize their own needs and desires without regard for the needs of others.

Still, others may find it difficult to relax and enjoy the present moment, always feeling like they must do more or achieve more to be worthy. This may result from a childhood in which they felt pressure to succeed or constantly strive for more.

Some individuals may become stuck in a state of feeling like a helpless victim, unable to take control of their lives and constantly at the mercy of external circumstances. This can result from a childhood in which they felt a lack of control and agency and may have developed a sense of learned helplessness as a coping mechanism.

Regardless of its specific form, this constant sense of dissatisfaction and inadequacy can make it difficult for individuals to find true contentment and happiness in their lives. They may feel like something is always wrong, that they are not enough, and that their lives are not enough, leading to a constant sense of worry and anxiety.

Let's say, for example, that you are ten years old and often see your parents arguing over house duties. They continuously blame each other for things and pass remarks such as, "You were supposed to take the kid to school" and "You were supposed to make dinner while I took care of the kid." You will blame yourself for their tussles, thinking you are the reason everything is going wrong in the house.

If your father is going through some work issues and not spending enough time with you or playing the weekend game of scrabble with you, you will think it is because you're unbearable or unlovable instead of thinking that maybe they have things going on in their life and are just busy. You feel like everything is your fault, and it all would have been better if you just "weren't in the picture."

These thoughts and ideas do not leave you even if you have grown up and are doing well for yourself. You will start having flashbacks to certain events and find connections in every little thing. If your friend is distant because she is busy preparing for her exams, you start believing that she is just avoiding you because you are not fun enough to be around, just like your father did when you were young.

Or if your romantic partner starts being a little upset due to a depressive episode, you will believe that it is again your fault that they are feeling this way and distancing themselves from you. This rejection will have you doubting yourself all over again, and you will start feeling that it is you that is just not wired right; you cannot make them happy enough, just like you were never enough for your parents. You will think that you are incapable of being a good child to your parents, a friend, or even a lover.

Childhood emotional scars can be akin to carrying a heavy load on one's back, symbolizing the weight of the pain and its impact on one's life. When a person's inner child has been hurt, it can leave a wound that lingers and haunts them for years. This pain often results from a profound sense of emptiness, a feeling of helplessness and hopelessness that seems to have no end. They may feel as though they are living a false life, devoid of excitement and joy, as if they're simply going through the motions of existence. This deep sense of disconnection between themselves and others can be devastating.

You may feel a compulsive urge to conceal your emotions, stifling your sobs and feigning a smile even when everything is far from okay. Conflict avoidance may be a constant struggle as you opt for the easiest path to escape uncomfortable situations. You may judge your worth based on your accomplishments and triumphs, viewing yourself as either exceptional or inadequate, with no middle ground.

The slightest criticism can trigger a downward spiral, causing you to retreat, crumble, or lash out in anger. As a people-pleaser, decision-making on your own may be a daunting task; you always seek validation and approval from others. Establishing and maintaining healthy boundaries, particularly with those who have significantly impacted your life, such as your parents or romantic partners, may be a constant battle.

But it's not just emotional pain that can stem from a wounded inner child. So often, it manifests itself in physical ways as well. Anxiety, depression, addiction, eating disorders, and C-PTSD are just some of the mental health issues that can arise. And even physical conditions like migraines, chronic fatigue syndrome, and fibromyalgia have been linked to the trauma of a hurt inner child.

These are all signs that your inner child is crying out for help, trying to communicate something crucial to you. They are trying to tell you that they need healing, that they need to be heard, and that they need to be loved.

If the inner child has lived through experiences of instability, uncertainty, or danger, it may hinder a person's ability to make positive changes in their life. They may feel afraid of trying new things, but at the same time, they want to move forward and break free from these limitations. This inner conflict can be challenging to overcome, but it is a critical step toward healing and growth.

Consider how your childhood experiences may be impacting your current relationships. Do you struggle to trust others, form close bonds, or communicate your needs and feelings? Are you prone to repeating patterns of behavior that keep you stuck in negative or unhealthy relationships? Are there areas where you may feel stuck, stagnant, or unfulfilled in your personal or professional life?

The wounded child within us is a desperate plea for help, a cry for love and care. But we must have the courage to face and embrace the pain, heal the wounds, and find peace. The journey is not an easy one, but the reward is immeasurable. Here are some signs that suggest you need to heal that little guy within you.

Self-Abandonment, the Emotional Root of Self Sabotage

Children are hard-wired to seek approval and validation from their parents. And if we do not receive the words we so desperately need, a self-sabotage pattern starts early in our developmental stage as a survival mechanism. This violation causes you to view the world badly and believe you do not deserve success and happiness.

Have you ever stalled your doctor's appointment? Not showed up to a job interview? Skipped your medications? Rejected that cute guy or girl that is the kindest person you have ever met? You keep being the hurdle in the path of your life, not letting yourself climb the ladder even though you are ready. You are ready to move forward.

You are ready for that nice job with health insurance and bonuses. You are ready to have a healthy body. You are ready to be in the best shape of your life. You are ready for a partner that is funny, kind, and knows how to take care of you. But your inner child isn't. It is still wounded and is scared that you will not be able to do well. Your inner child is trying to save you from rejection and embarrassment. It is trying to save you from yourself.

There are many ways you can sabotage yourself. You may often "forget" things or believe you are too lazy to get things done. You keep losing your cool on the tiniest things, constantly getting into arguments and fights. The fear of success and what others might think of you have settled so deep that you do not let yourself be happy. There seems to be no match between your values and your behavior. If this describes you, your inner child needs your attention.

Overreacting On Small Things

Do you find yourself making a big fuss over the smallest things? You can't have a hold over your emotions. Everything you feel shows, and every emotion you go through appears on your face.

Sometimes, we may not remember the specific events from our childhood that caused us harm, but they can still leave a lasting impact on our lives. To better understand these hidden wounds, it's important to pay attention to our reactions and emotions in certain situations.

If we find ourselves feeling overly upset, angry, or hurt in response to events that seem minor or inconsequential, this could be a sign that we have unresolved emotional wounds from our past. For instance, feeling intense anger or frustration when someone does not reply to our text messages on time even though they are busy could indicate that our need for attention was not met when we were young. This could result in a deep-seated wound that we carry with us into adulthood and which manifests in overreactions to similar situations.

The outburst is not the worst part; it is the guilt that follows. The upside of being an emotional rollercoaster is that you cannot keep your feelings and opinions to yourself. You end up truth bombing, pouring out your feelings, and then regretting hurting others with your words. You feel as though you are emotionally weak, always creating scenarios and bringing drama everywhere you go.

Filling the Void with Alcohol and Drugs

Do you often run to bars and clubs to douse yourself in drugs and liquor every time you feel some "bad emotions?" Instead of finding out why you are feeling the way you are and running from your emotions, you chose to neglect them. You are so scared of confronting yourself that you would rather drink away your own problems or harm yourself in other ways, such as self-harm and gaming addictions, anything you can do to detach yourself from reality.

You find these unhealthy coping mechanisms, so you do not have to face your feelings. You tire yourself, keeping your mind so busy that it doesn't have a moment to think or feel anything. The truth is much deeper than the pit of despair you have dug for yourself. You are not addicted to these activities but rather the feeling of running away from reality.

If you resonate with these signs, your inner child is calling out for your help. Instead of denying yourself emotions and feelings, talk to your inner child and find out what is wrong. Discover why you are avoiding going into your past. What are you hiding from yourself?

Living Under a Dark Cloud

Were you often surrounded by adults that made you feel down? Guilt trapping, gaslighting, false blaming, and shaming you in subtle and not-so-subtle ways? If you feel like a voice is constantly bullying you and feeding you negative thoughts inside your head, it may be due to those adults who did the same. What you hear and see imprints subconsciously on you, making your view of the world black and white. You live with constant anxiety and depression, never feeling like you are enough.

You need to confront this inner bully and understand that not everything they say is true. You must nurture and love your inner child to be confident and stand up for yourself. Try picturing the image of you as a kid whenever you say something bad to yourself. Would you like them to hear that about you? Would you like their glistening eyes and adorable smile to vanish? Feed them kind words instead. Words that they have been longing to hear, love that they have been waiting to feel. Let them know they are valued and that you are grateful to them.

Living For Others

As a people-pleaser, you may have experienced feeling like your only purpose in life is to make others happy. This can be a result of past events or people in your childhood who conditioned you to believe that your self-worth is tied to the happiness of others. When this happens, you may feel unhappy if you can't bring joy to those around you.

However, it's important to recognize that this is a result of emotional scars that have been left on your inner child. Continuously apologizing and feeling like you've done something wrong is another indication of these past experiences.

While being helpful and pleasing to others is not necessarily bad, it turns problematic when it becomes a compulsion, something you crave like a drug. As adults, it's essential that we find ways to make ourselves feel good and valuable, rather than relying on others for validation. Inner-child psychology explores these concepts, and the inner-child theory is still accepted by many in the field of psychology today.

Always Feeling Guilty

The feeling of constantly needing to apologize and believing that you have done something wrong clearly indicates deep-seated insecurities and self-doubt stemming from your childhood. It's likely that someone who played a significant role in your life, such as a parent, relative, or caregiver, made you feel guilty and ashamed for simply being who you are. They may have blamed you for their own difficulties, such as the cost of raising you, the effort to take you to school, or the time spent talking to you.

This type of emotional abuse can have a lasting impact on a child's sense of self-worth and self-esteem. Your inner child, who once had a pure and innocent view of the world, was made to believe that they were inherently flawed and that everything they did was wrong. This distorted belief has become a part of their inner narrative and continues to haunt them even into adulthood.

It's important to acknowledge and validate the pain that you have experienced and to understand that you were never the problem. You were never to blame for the difficulties of others, and you deserve love, respect, and acceptance just as you are.

Stuck in a Rough Patch

Do you often feel like you are not worthy of love? Do you keep getting into relationships that are not good for you? Do you keep finding partners that are abusive, addicted, or not healthy? Do you constantly chase after emotionally unavailable people? If you keep getting yourself into toxic situations, as Halsey says, you are bad at love, which could be a sign that your inner child has been deeply wounded. It's possible that you haven't fully recognized the pattern in your relationships, but the individuals who have taken advantage of your love and trust and caused you harm are reflections of the negative relationship dynamics you are unconsciously drawn to.

It's not uncommon for individuals who have experienced trauma in their childhood to struggle with regulating their emotions, leading to outbursts of anger and even abusive behavior towards their partners. However, when you consistently find yourself in relationships with partners who mirror the abuse and negativity you have experienced, it could be a manifestation of past traumas resurfacing.

The wounds from your past can be like shackles that keep you from experiencing the love and happiness you so deserve. Your childhood scars cost you your love life. You either completely turn your head away from love, not getting into any relationship, get into a series of bad relationships, or are too clingy and needy with your partners. You never feel satisfied with anything and subconsciously sabotage your chance at finding real love. You fight a lot and constantly second-guess everything they say or do. You have trust issues with everyone, including your own family.

Perhaps your childhood was marked by witnessing or experiencing abuse at the hands of your parents, causing deep emotional wounds that have never fully healed. It's crucial to understand this connection and seek support in addressing these traumatic experiences to break the cycle and create healthier relationships for yourself in the future.

Holding Off from Trying New Things

When it comes to new experiences, it's common to feel a touch of nervousness or uncertainty. This is a natural response to stepping outside of our comfort zones. However, when that fear becomes so intense that it holds us back from trying new things, it can be a sign of something deeper. It's possible that you experienced a traumatic event in your childhood that has left a lasting impact on you.

For example, suppose you saved up and bought your dream dress for your prom event, and it turned out almost exactly how you imagined, but you accidentally burned it while steaming. And instead of comfort and support, your parents made fun of you for being so silly, failing to comfort you. Or the time you were scared of going on that roller coaster that looked like death, and your parents and siblings laughed at you, calling you a "chicken." These kinds of experiences can leave a deep imprint on a child's mind and have long-lasting effects on their emotions and behaviors.

As an adult, you may struggle to shake off that fear and anxiety when faced with new experiences. Even something as simple as taking a different route to work can trigger feelings of intense discomfort and unease. When pushed into new activities, you may become snappy and argumentative, unable to cope with the anxiety and stress of trying something new.

It's important to remember that these reactions are not your fault and are likely rooted in past experiences that have shaped your perception of the world. By acknowledging these fears and working through them, you can reclaim your confidence and embrace new experiences without feeling overwhelmed or trapped by fear.

"It sounds corny, but I've promised my inner child that never again will I ever abandon myself for anything or anyone else again."

- Wynonna Judd

CHAPTER 3: WHY DO WE LOSE CONNECTION WITH OUR INNER CHILD?

When we are kids, we like to build our own fantasy worlds. We are not concerned with what is real and what is fake. Then, suddenly, we have to "fend for ourselves," have a sleepover for the last time, and play for the last time.

As we grow older, we can no longer rely on the adults in our lives. Well, how could we? We are now the adults in our lives. We must act and take control of our lives before they start to control us. We feel the pressure to act maturely, and in that, we suppress our fearless, playful, happy side. Instead of telling things like they are, we put a filter on life. We grow shyer and keep to ourselves more, afraid to reveal ourselves to the world. Fear of rejection engulfs us and puts a lock on our tongues, having us spend our lives holding back.

"The false self, or ego, is who we are when the Adult chooses the intent to protect and disconnects from the Inner Child. The unloving Adult and the unloved abandoned Child are the two faces of the ego."

- Margaret Paul

We need to let our true self shine! Everyone deserves to speak their mind and act out their wishes without thinking, "What will people say?"

The pain from childhood experiences can manifest in adulthood as immaturity, low self-esteem, boundary issues, and other challenges. This can lead to difficulty managing emotions such as resentment, rage, addiction, emotional swings, and challenges with intimacy.

Suppressing childhood pain doesn't make it disappear. Instead, it can resurface in adulthood, causing distress in personal relationships and making it difficult to meet your needs. Focusing on healing your inner child can help address these issues. Here are a few reasons why our inner child might be having a tough time.

Childhood Experiences

Our childhood experiences can significantly impact our emotional development and sense of self. Difficult or traumatic experiences, such as abuse, neglect, or loss, can cause us to disconnect from our emotions and inner child as a coping mechanism to protect ourselves from further pain or hurt. We may suppress or numb our feelings to survive these experiences. As a result, we may lose connection with our inner child and our natural sense of curiosity, playfulness, and vulnerability.

Take some time to reflect on your childhood experiences. Did you feel loved, supported, and nurtured by your caregivers? Were there any significant losses, traumas, or disappointments that impacted you? Did you feel safe, secure, and valued growing up?

Societal Expectations

As we grow up, we may feel pressure to conform to societal expectations and "act our age." This can involve suppressing our natural sense of playfulness and curiosity in favor of more "serious" or "mature" behaviors. We may feel that it is not acceptable or appropriate to express or engage in childlike behaviors as adults. This can cause us to lose connection with our inner child, sense of authenticity, and connection to our true selves.

Life Stressors

As adults, we may face a range of stressors that can cause us to feel overwhelmed or preoccupied. These stressors include work, relationships, financial responsibilities, and other demands on our time and energy. These demands can make finding time and space to connect with our inner child and the present moment difficult. We may feel overwhelmed by worry or fear, which can cause us to lose connection with our inner child.

Lack of Opportunities

As adults, we may have fewer opportunities to engage in activities that allow us to connect with our inner child, such as playing or creating. We may not prioritize these activities or have the time or resources to pursue them.

Bullying and Rejection

Children who experience bullying, rejection, or exclusion from peers may develop a sense of shame, self-doubt, and inadequacy. These experiences can also affect their social skills, self-esteem, and sense of belonging.

Unmet Childhood Needs

Children who do not receive the emotional support, validation, and nurturing they need to develop a healthy sense of self may struggle with feelings of emptiness, loneliness, and a lack of self-worth. This can lead to difficulty forming healthy relationships and a sense of direction in life.

Abuse and Neglect

One of the most common causes of a wounded inner child is physical, emotional, or sexual abuse. Children who experience abuse may develop feelings of shame, guilt, low self-esteem, and a sense of helplessness or powerlessness. Neglect, or a lack of adequate care or attention, can also be a source of emotional pain for children and leave them feeling unloved or unworthy.

Unhappy Home

Children who grow up in households with high levels of conflict or who experience the divorce or separation of their parents may struggle with feelings of abandonment, betrayal, or loss.

These experiences can leave them with a sense of insecurity and instability in their relationships and overall sense of self.

Traumatic Incidents

Traumatic events such as accidents, illness, or natural disasters can also cause emotional wounds in children. Trauma can disrupt a child's sense of safety and security, leaving them fearful, anxious, and vulnerable.

Love on Condition

If a caregiver only shows love and affection when the child meets certain conditions or expectations, such as achieving good grades or behaving in a certain way, it can lead to feelings of unworthiness in the child. The child may start to believe that they only deserve love and affection when they meet these conditions and may feel rejected or unloved when they don't.

Cultural Factors

Cultural factors such as poverty, discrimination, or social stigma can contribute to inner child hurt. Children who grow up in marginalized communities may experience feelings of shame, inferiority, and a lack of belonging.

Chronic Stress

Chronic stress, such as living in poverty or experiencing ongoing conflict, can cause emotional pain and leave a child feeling helpless and overwhelmed. Children living in war-torn or conflict-ridden areas may experience ongoing stress and trauma.

Invalidation

Dismissing or denying a child's feelings, experiences, or opinions can leave them feeling unimportant and unseen. When a child's feelings and experiences are not validated, they may struggle with isolation and disconnection from others, making it difficult to develop healthy coping mechanisms and positive relationships.

Negative Self-Perception

Our negative self-perception can also cause us to disconnect from our inner child. We may feel unworthy or incapable of experiencing joy or vulnerability. We may believe that we do not deserve playfulness or fun or need to be "perfect" to be loved and accepted. These negative beliefs can prevent us from fully embracing our inner child and our range of emotions.

Loss

As we grow up, we may experience loss in various forms, such as losing a loved one, ending a relationship, or losing a dream or opportunity. These experiences can be emotionally painful and can cause us to disconnect from our inner child to cope with the pain. We may suppress our emotions or engage in unhealthy behaviors to numb the pain.

Many factors can contribute to a loss of connection with our inner child. The causes of a wounded inner child are varied and complex and can have lasting effects on a person's emotional and psychological well-being. Recognizing and addressing the emotional wounds of the past can be an important step in healing and moving toward a healthier, happier, and more fulfilling life.

It's important to be aware of these influences and find ways to rekindle and embrace our inner child to maintain a sense of balance and well-being.

CHAPTER 4: WHAT ARE THE BENEFITS OF RECONNECTING WITH OUR INNER CHILD?

You know what they say: "You can't choose your family, but you can choose your adult self!" And it's true; a big part of who we are today is based on our childhood experiences. How we were raised, the care we received, and even the things we learned to fear all greatly shaped us into the adults we are today. And even though we've grown up and left childhood behind, we still carry all that conditioning with us, which can influence our everyday decisions.

You know, sometimes our inner child can be a real pooper. It can represent all those negative experiences and emotions from our childhood, like neglect, abuse, or trauma. But just because our inner child has some baggage doesn't mean we can't help them unpack it! Healing our inner child can be crucial to dealing with and resolving those past experiences. It's like having a therapy session with the younger version of yourself and helping them understand and process what happened.

But here's the good news: by reconnecting with our inner child, we can heal those old wounds and change how we think about things. It's like hitting the reset button on our brain and starting fresh! There are many ways to connect with our inner child, like journaling, meditation, and even playtime. We can invite more joy and happiness into our everyday lives by releasing those childhood anxieties and fears. So, let's take some time to reconnect with our inner child and give them the love and care they deserve so they can grow up to be a happier and healthier adult!

"Our problem is not that as children our needs were unmet, but that as adults they are still unmourned!"

- David Richo

It's important to remember that our parents are human, and they, too, make mistakes, even though they did their best to raise us. I've found that reminding myself of this helps me have more compassion for them and myself. Even though I understand that it doesn't erase the pain and trauma from my childhood.

For a long time, I held onto that pain, and it caused me to harbor resentments, feel like a victim, and be stuck in a cycle of sadness. But when I started working on my inner child, I was able to be kind and compassionate toward the wounds she had suffered. I could nurture and care for her; in doing so, I could heal myself as an adult. It's amazing how the healing of our inner child can also bring healing to our adult selves.

There is research to support the idea that connecting with your inner child can be beneficial for your emotional well-being and overall health. For example, a published in the International Journal of Art Therapy found that engaging in activities that allow you to tap into your inner child, such as play and creativity, can increase positive emotions and your sense of personal growth.

Another published in the International Journal of Qualitative Studies on Health and Well-Being found that engaging in activities that allow you to reconnect with your inner child, such as hobbies and creative pursuits, can lead to increased well-being and a greater sense of meaning and purpose in life.

To quote Dr. Venetia Leonidaki, an expert psychologist trained in various forms of psychotherapy:

"Connecting with your inner child can put you in touch with a wider range of emotions, boost your creativity, enhance your desire to have fun, and help you feel more light-hearted. It can also reduce feelings of emotional numbness and disconnection and make you more aware of suppressed negative emotions, which could have made you more prone to mental health difficulties. If there are any wounds from your childhood that need healing, reconnecting with your inner child could give you the opportunity to work through them. Finally, you could end up with a complete sense of who you are by connecting different parts of yourself together"

Additionally, your inner child holds all your unmet needs and desires from childhood. When you're able to identify and meet these needs, it can lead to a greater sense of self-awareness and fulfillment.

Working on your inner child can also help you let go of limiting beliefs and patterns that may hold you back. It allows you to tap into your inner wisdom and creativity and can lead to a more positive and authentic expression of self.

Reasons Why You Should Reconnect with Your Inner Child

Imagine a precious, innocent child who's been hurt but is still trying to make their way in this big, confusing world. That child still lives within you, and whenever something important is threatened, or you feel disrespected, that inner child comes out in full force, flooding you with intense emotions like fear, hurt, and shame, often disguised as anger. It's not your fault; this is just the child's way of coping and feeling safe.

But when our wounded child takes over, it often triggers the same in others, leading to a never-ending cycle of emotional outbursts. However, once you become aware of your wounded child and recognize when it's triggered, you can choose to react differently. By showing compassion and understanding towards yourself and others, you can break the cycle and transform your relationships and overall life experience.

Think of it this way: if you faced a sad, scared, or angry child right now, would you ignore or berate them? No, you would show them kindness and understanding. Your inner child deserves the same treatment. Remember, everyone around you is harboring their own wounded child, even those who seem confident and successful. By becoming aware of this and having compassion for others, you can ease any fear and improve your relationships with everyone.

This is why it is so important to care for and nurture your inner child and bring it back to the happy, carefree self that it used to be. Make it feel loved and secure, so it no longer is a barrier in your life. Here are a few things you can do to rekindle that fun, happy spirit in you.

Understand Who You Are

Connecting with your inner child can help you feel more connected to your past and sense of identity. Your inner child represents the part of you connected to your childhood experiences, memories, and emotions. Think of it this way; your inner child is like the "before" picture in a before-and-after transformation.

By embracing your inner child, you're completing the transformation and understanding who you are and where you come from. You can feel like you've traveled back in time and reconnected with your past and sense of identity.

Inner-child work can also help us to develop self-compassion and self-awareness, which can further aid in understanding our triggers and emotions.

A New Level of Awareness

Inner-child work can help us to understand the reasons behind our emotions, such as why we feel anxious or stressed in certain situations. By understanding the root cause of our emotions, we can learn to manage them better and reduce the intensity of our emotional responses.

"If we learn to dissociate from the pain of our reality, we can survive a childhood of tremendous betrayal, sadness, pain, and fear. But dissociation... from pain is not selective; we inevitably disconnect even from the joy of being alive."

- Daniel Siegel

Working on our inner child can feel like opening the door to a whole new world. For a long time, I didn't even realize how much my inner child influenced my thoughts, feelings, and actions as an adult. But working with a trauma therapist helped me understand that my inner child was still there, holding onto old fears and insecurities from my childhood.

For example, I used to feel really insecure about standing up for myself and speaking my mind. But as I worked on my inner child, I realized that this fear was rooted in my childhood experiences where I couldn't have my own opinions or voice. So, I internalized that and stopped allowing myself to be assertive.

Reconnect With Your Passions

When you were a child, what profession did you dream of pursuing? Are you currently working in that field, or have you veered in a different direction?

It is important to consider that most of our lives are spent in the workplace. Therefore, it is essential to have a career that brings satisfaction and fulfillment. Inner child work can assist in uncovering creative ways to pursue one's passions, even if it means finding ways to incorporate them into your current job or finding a side hustle.

For example, if you have always dreamed of being an actor but currently work a 9-5 job, quitting your job and moving to Hollywood may not be practical, but you can explore options such as shooting video auditions from home after hours. Inner-child work can help you reconnect with your passions and find ways to bring them into your current life rather than feeling like you have to give up on them.

Go With the Flow

When was the last time you indulged in a spontaneous weekend road trip with your loved one or engaged in a random slow dance in your living room simply for the joy of it? Keeping your inner child alive can help to tap into your spontaneous and carefree side. A child does not worry about who might be listening when their favorite song comes on; they sing it with all the energy and enthusiasm they possess.

Similarly, if you let go of your inhibitions, engage in spontaneous activities, and let loose, you may find that it leads to greater happiness and well-being. For example, turn your car into a "recording studio" and sing at the top of your lungs to your favorite songs during a road trip. Inner child work can help bring back that sense of freedom and joy often lost as we grow older and become more concerned with societal expectations and norms.

Conquer Your Fears

When we think of children, we often imagine them as full of wonder and eager to discover the world around them. They are not afraid to get their hands dirty and try new things; they are full of energy and enthusiasm. This childlike curiosity and willingness to take risks can also be valuable in adult life. Inner-child work is a practice that involves reconnecting with this sense of wonder and curiosity that we had as children. By tapping into this inner child, you can learn to approach life and opportunities with a sense of wonder and excitement.

While it is important to consider the potential downsides and risks of any decision, such as starting a business without enough capital or investing in a new venture without proper research, inner-child work can help you approach these decisions with excitement and possibility. It can encourage taking healthy risks, such as trying out a new hobby, taking a class, or traveling to a new place. Inner-child work can help you see the world in a new way and approach opportunities with renewed excitement and curiosity.

Be Your Best Self

Maintaining a sense of childlike wonder and playfulness in your life can bring a great deal of joy and laughter. By tapping into your inner child, you may laugh harder and more often, releasing endorphins and making you feel happier. This can also have physical benefits, such as toning your abdominal muscles. When facing difficult or challenging situations, try approaching them with a sense of curiosity and playfulness, as a child might. You may find that what seemed like a daunting task is actually an enjoyable experience in disguise.

By delving into this aspect of ourselves, we can learn to be kinder and more compassionate towards ourselves and others. It can also give us a new perspective on how to live a more fulfilling life.

The Domino Effect

When we don't take the time to address and heal from past hurts, it can lead to some pretty destructive behaviors. For example, this can include being a workaholic, turning to alcohol for comfort, or even being racist. And it's not just bad for us; it can also affect the people around us and the world as a whole.

It's important to remember that healing our inner child isn't just about us; it's about healing generations. When we take the time to heal ourselves, it can positively impact the world. It's like a domino effect. By healing ourselves, we're also helping to heal others. It's a process called coregulation, and it's pretty powerful.

Understand Your Relationships

If you find yourself repeatedly drawn to the same type of person or struggling to break old, toxic behavior patterns, inner-child work may be an effective tool in understanding and addressing these issues. Inner child work is a therapeutic approach that focuses on exploring and understanding the emotional and psychological experiences of childhood to gain insight into the origin of current maladaptive behaviors.

By recognizing the negative impact of these behaviors, which may have been acquired in childhood, individuals can begin the process of recovery and healing. It is important to understand that simply recognizing the root cause of these self-sabotaging actions is often enough to put the necessary checks in place to prevent them from happening again.

Create a Bridge

Inner-child work can help create a more resilient bridge between the two brain hemispheres by addressing and healing past traumas and negative experiences that may have caused a disconnection or imbalance. This can lead to improved cognitive function and the ability to access multiple functions by allowing the individual to understand and process the emotions and memories associated with past traumas or negative experiences. It also helps the individual to develop a more nurturing and supportive inner parent that can guide and support their inner child. Additionally, it creates a safe space for the individual to share and express their feelings. Due to all these reasons, inner-child work can help to reduce stress and anxiety, which can help to re-balance the brain hemispheres.

You Are Enough

One of the benefits of this practice is that it can help to decrease feelings of shame and inadequacy. This is because many negative beliefs we hold about ourselves, such as "I'm not good enough" or "I'm not worthy," often stem from traumatic experiences or messages we received during childhood. By reconnecting with our inner child, we can understand the root causes of these negative beliefs and start the healing process.

Through inner-child work, we can understand how these negative beliefs about ourselves were formed and how they have affected us throughout our lives. By acknowledging the past traumas and experiences that shaped our beliefs, we can start letting go of these negative thoughts and embrace self-love and acceptance. Inner-child work helps us reconnect with our true selves and inner child and see ourselves with compassion and understanding.

Let Go of the Past

Sometimes our inner child can hold onto some heavy stuff from our childhood. We might not have fully addressed or even acknowledged unresolved issues or traumas. If we don't take the time to work through our pain, it will keep popping up differently. And it's not uncommon that these memories and emotions can be related to difficult or painful experiences that we have gone through. It can be hard to process and understand these experiences, but working with your inner child can help you tap into and address these unresolved issues in a healthy way.

It's like deep diving into the past and working through these issues with kindness and compassion. It's not going to be easy, but it's worth it. By acknowledging and working through these issues, you can start to heal and move forward healthily. And you might be surprised how much better you'll feel once you've given your inner child the attention they need. It's going to be a journey worth taking.

Understand Your Emotional Triggers

Inner-child work helps increase awareness of triggers by allowing us to gain insight into unresolved emotions and traumas from our childhood. Through inner-child work, we can identify patterns and experiences from our past that may be impacting our current emotional state. This increased awareness can help us to understand why certain triggers may elicit such a strong emotional response, such as flooding or freezing.

For example, if someone has experienced trauma in their childhood, their inner child may still hold onto that trauma and fear, which can lead to an emotional flood or freeze response when triggered. Through inner-child work, that person can identify the source of the trauma, process it, and release it, which can help to reduce the intensity of the emotional response to triggers.

Get a Sense of Safety

Inner-child work helps establish a sense of safety within the body and nervous system by addressing unresolved emotions and traumas from childhood. When we experience traumatic events, our body and nervous system can become hypervigilant and respond to present-day stressors as if they were still in danger.

"We all have made the mistake of thinking someone else can be our healer, our thriller, our filling. It takes a long time to find it is not so, mostly because we project the wound outside ourselves instead of ministering to it within.

Inner-child work allows us to process and release these unresolved emotions, which can help to calm the nervous system and create a sense of safety within the body.

Give Wings to Your Imagination

When we were kids, things were pretty simple. We had fun, we played, and we didn't have a care in the world. We were always coming up with new ideas, stories, and games. But as we grow older, we may focus more on practicality and lose touch with that sense of imagination and creativity. It can be as simple as taking a break from adulting and doing something that you used to enjoy as a kid, like coloring or playing with toys, or even just allowing yourself to be in the moment and enjoy it without feeling guilty. Even if you work in a field that is not traditionally considered "creative," such as finance or engineering, incorporating creativity into your work can add a unique element to your daily routine.

Whether coloring in a book, making a fun bracelet, or painting a birdhouse, let yourself have fun and enjoy the process without worrying about the result. Remember, it's not about creating something perfect; it's about enjoying the journey. By reconnecting with our inner child, we can tap into that natural creativity and imagination and use it to come up with new ideas, solve problems in unique ways, and generally approach life with a fresh perspective.

Learn to Trust Others

One thing that many people in recovery have in common is that they tend to keep to themselves and push away even their closest loved ones. And it's not just a recovery thing; it's also something that can happen to people who had a tough childhood, like being abandoned. They might think that if they keep their distance, they'll avoid getting hurt again.

What they will get from this journey is the lesson that human interaction is important.

Building trust and sharing your journey with others is hard when you haven't sorted out the past. But to move forward and build healthy relationships, it's important to work through the past and learn to trust again.

The Scientific Side

Inner-child work can help to activate the right brain, which is associated with creativity, emotions, imagination, and intuition. The right brain is also responsible for non-verbal communication, such as body language, facial expressions, and tone of voice. By reconnecting with our inner child, we can tap into the more intuitive and creative aspects of our personality, which can help to enhance our ability to express ourselves and understand others.

The right brain is also connected to the limbic system, which is responsible for our emotional processing and regulation. Inner-child work can help regulate our emotions and release unresolved traumas, reducing the intensity of our emotional response to triggers.

On the other hand, inner-child work can also support the left brain, which is responsible for logic, reason, language, and analytic thinking. By understanding our emotions and triggers, we can better understand ourselves, which can help improve our logical and analytical thinking. This can lead to better decision-making, problem-solving, and effective communication.

Inner-child work can also help balance the two sides of the brain by allowing us to express our emotions and intuition healthily, leading to better decision-making, problem-solving, and effective communication. By better understanding ourselves, we can also improve our ability to understand others and communicate with them more effectively.

Freeing that wounded inner child can help you be more present in the moment and enjoy life more fully. Children live in the present and are not as weighed down by the past or worried about the future as adults can be. By embracing your inner child, you can learn to let go of these distractions and focus on what is happening here and now.

Reconnecting with your inner child can be a real game-changer. It can help you feel more connected to your past, bring back that sense of playfulness and creativity you had as a child, help you process any unresolved issues or traumas from your childhood, make you feel more spontaneous and carefree, and allow you to be more present and enjoy life more fully.

It's like giving your adult self a big hug from your inner child. And it's a win-win situation because not only will you be doing something good for yourself but also for your inner child, who needs to be acknowledged, listened to, and loved. So, why not try it and reconnect with your inner child? It could be a healing and enriching experience that could positively impact your overall well-being.

As people grow up, they bring with them both good and bad memories from their childhood. For many young adults, their struggles come from traumatic experiences they endured during their childhood. These traumas can manifest in various forms, such as anxiety, depression, substance abuse, or other mental health concerns.

The trauma can take many forms, including physical, sexual, or verbal abuse, and can range from a single traumatic event to ongoing, complex trauma. In many cases, the trauma is related to relationships, stemming from a broken bond with a parent or caretaker. This can result in deep, long-lasting psychological wounds.

Children who have faced neglect or rejection may use numbing and disconnecting from their emotions as a way to cope with intense pain. As a result, they may repress feelings of anger or grief, leaving their inner child to hold onto these difficult emotions.

PART 2 - HOW CAN WE RECONNECT WITH OUR INNER CHILD?

CHAPTER 5: HOW CAN WE RECONNECT WITH OUR INNER CHILD?

S uppressing or avoiding the pain of the past will not make it disappear, and it can manifest in various forms, such as relationship difficulties or struggles in fulfilling one's own needs. To address these issues, it is important to work towards healing the inner child.

"We don't stop playing because we grow old; we grow old because we stop playing."

-George Bernard Shaw

The process of inner child work can seem daunting, but it's important to remember that it's not much different from self-care. It's about being compassionate and nurturing towards yourself, just like a parent would be. It's about being mindful of your thoughts, emotions, and needs and taking the necessary steps to heal any pain or trauma from your childhood. The process of healing the inner child can be time-consuming, but here are some more detailed tips to get started:

Go Down the Memory Lane

Inner-child work is a form of self-exploration and healing that helps individuals reconnect with their inner child, the part of themselves that holds their childhood memories, emotions, and experiences. The inner child is often associated with our sense of innocence, spontaneity, and playfulness, which can be lost or suppressed as we grow older.

To start the inner-child work process, one can begin by exploring memories, experiences, and emotions. This can be done by looking through old photo albums and childhood diaries or reaching out to friends and family from their childhood. As memories are revisited, it's important to acknowledge and process any painful memories that may surface.

Inner-child work involves addressing and healing these emotional wounds, which can be done through sharing them with a loved one, expressing them through creative outlets, or discussing them with a therapist. Take some time to think about your childhood experiences and how they may have shaped you. Consider any difficult experiences or emotions you may have had and how you coped with them.

On the other hand, exploring memories may also bring back feelings of strength, hope, and positivity. If this is the case, try to channel these traits in your present life and embrace the playfulness, optimism, and joy your inner child embodies.

Be Kind to Yourself

The messages we receive during childhood can significantly impact our beliefs, emotions, and behaviors as adults. For example, if a child is raised in an environment where competition is emphasized and they are constantly compared to others, they may develop feelings of inadequacy and self-doubt as an adult. On the other hand, if a child experiences emotional neglect from their parents, they may seek out emotionally unavailable partners in adulthood as it feels familiar to them.

"When our Inner Child feels consistently unloved by our Inner Adult, the Child's false beliefs, adopted in childhood when parents

were unloving, are reinforced—beliefs that we are bad, wrong, unlovable, unimportant, inadequate, defective in some way."

- Margaret Paul

To heal the wounds of the past, it is essential to speak to ourselves with compassion and kindness. This can involve recognizing and reframing negative messages and beliefs we received in the past and replacing them with positive affirmations such as "I am worthy," "I am capable," and "I am enough." It may feel strange, but these words of encouragement can bring comfort and peace.

Another way to heal the past is to write down your thoughts from the perspective of your inner child. Express your innermost worries and pain. Reflect on how this makes you feel and if it brings any relief. Sometimes, all we need is to be heard and seen to begin the healing process.

Engage in Activities That Bring You Joy

Reconnecting with our inner child can be liberating and bring a sense of joy and freedom. Activities we enjoyed as children, such as playing on the swings, rollerblading, or jumping into a pool with our clothes on, can bring back a sense of nostalgia and remind us of the carefree days of our childhood.

As adults, we often prioritize responsibilities and obligations over activities that bring us pure joy and pleasure. We may even give up activities we used to enjoy, viewing them as "childish" or "not useful." However, it is essential to remember that engaging in activities that bring us joy is essential for our overall well-being.

Find activities that allow you to tap into your playfulness and creativity, such as creating art, dancing, or playing music. Whether it's something as simple as going for a hike ride, drawing, or playing an instrument, revisiting activities we loved as children can be a refreshing and invigorating experience. It's a reminder that we don't always have to be serious and mature and that it's okay to let go and have fun.

Go ahead and indulge in activities that bring you joy and remind you of your childhood, like playing with Play-Doh, coloring, or jumping on a trampoline. You'll not only have a blast but also gain valuable insights on how to live a happier, more balanced life.

Practice Mindfulness and Being Present

Have you ever noticed that being stressed or anxious can make you feel like you're stuck in your head and disconnected from your body? Well, a simple way to help is by taking a moment to focus on your breath and connect with your physical self.

Doing this helps us relax and step out of the constant stress and "fight or flight" mode that we can get stuck in as adults. It also allows us to be more present and curious about what's happening around us.

One way to do this is by taking a few deep breaths and paying attention to how your body feels. You can even put one hand on your chest and another on your belly to help you focus on your breath. Bring your attention to the present moment and observe your thoughts and feelings without judgment. This can help you become more aware of your inner child and better understand the thoughts and feelings driving your behavior.

While doing this, try to also note what you see, smell, hear, taste, and feel. It can be anything, like the color of the walls or the smell of your coffee. This helps to bring your attention to the present moment and away from any thoughts that might be causing stress.

Time to Get Messy

As adults, we are constantly pressured to have our life togeth-er. Always keep our home organized, beds made, clothes put away—you know, all the boring things. We cannot be messy as we are afraid of being judged. We do not play at the beach as we used to as kids, afraid we will get sand all over us. We don't go out in the rain, afraid of getting our clothes wet. We do not do anything that brought joy to us as kids.

Do not hold back from making a mess once in a while. Being a human is messy. Do not be afraid of the mud. Allow yourself to get lost in things that once brought you joy. Bring out that jewelry-making kit from when you were a kid. Or that race car set that you have stashed away in the attic. Bring out that makeup collection and spend your time doing your makeup. Sit with your kids, nieces, or nephews and play with Play-Doh. Stay in on a Sunday evening and bake. Sit on the front lawn, take out your art set, and paint. Do things that make you feel free. Sure, you will make a little mess that you must clean. But it will be so worth it.

Stop Filtering Everything

Besides being tiny, innocent, messy creatures, another factor that makes them a "kid" is that they do not have filters in their mouths. They cannot sense others' feelings as well as us, so they do not shy away from speaking the truth. We have all been victims of the truth spell. A kid called you out on something that took you by surprise. Or they told other people things you have wanted to say for a really long time.

Unlike adults, who keep their opinions and feelings locked in a box deep inside their minds. It must be tiring to keep everything together for the sake of others, right? Biting your lips so you do not say the wrong thing to someone, hurting yourself to please others. Never telling anyone how you feel, afraid to have burning, judgmental eyes land on you.

I am not asking you to lose the filter altogether. The world is not ready for that yet. Just practice speaking out for yourself. Be honest about how you are feeling. Tell that friend it wasn't really "okay" when he canceled plans on you right at the last moment. Tell your partner that you do not want to eat at a restaurant that you do not like. Tell your mother you do not appreciate the comment on your weight each time you meet her. Turn down that wedding invitation from a work colleague you do not like. Start small and work your way up from there. Speaking up is more powerful than being silent.

Connect With Nature

Remember how your father took you to the "wild outdoors" as a kid? You loved that time with your family—going out into the field, just running around, having the time of your life, camping in the summer vacations, and gazing at the stars as they passed you by. Taking a dip with your friends in that suspicious-looking lake. Dancing in the rain and jumping in the puddles to see the water splash. Walking home from school and admiring the flowers and trees that come your way. That is, until we grow up, put all of it behind us, and just get busy doing life.

Adults see life in tunnel vision, glued to their phones, rushing from home to work, work to home, and living in a monotonous cycle. It is time you take a moment for yourself. Push back your plans and take a walk in nature. Not to exercise but to remember that you do not have to rush everything. So, go for a real walk instead of an extensive hike to the mountaintop. Take in the scenery and let the cool breeze hit your face.

Close your eyes and listen to birds singing and chirping. Look up and notice how beautiful the sky is, how the stars twinkle in it. Look at how the kids enjoy themselves in the local park, free from all worries. Stop to smell the flowers and appreciate their beauty. Being in nature can be soothing and nourishing, and it can help you feel more connected to your inner self.

Spend Time With Those Tiny Humans

There is no better way to bring out that child within you than spending time with children themselves. Children can naturally embrace their inner child fully—the part of themselves that is curious, playful, and open to new experiences. They can fully engage with the world around them and find joy in small things. As adults, we often become more jaded and may not experience the same wonder and excitement in our daily lives.

However, by interacting and playing with our children, we can tap into our inner child and rediscover the joy and curiosity we may have lost over time. In this way, our children can remind us to live in the moment and find joy in the world around us. If you are not a parent, take time for your nieces and nephews the next time you go to your family reunion. Visit your friend with the kids. Get to their level and be a kid along with them. Spend time playing make-believe.

Play hide-and-seek with them, run around, and play video games or board games. Joke around with them. It is best to use your dad jokes here because, let's be real, adults do not enjoy them. Impart your knowledge, teach them new things, new games, and new words. Give life to their ridiculous ideas. They want to have pancakes for dinner? Sure, why not? Douse it in syrup and eat with them.

Next time someone asks you to babysit the little ones, don't hesitate to volunteer!

Awaken the Artist Within

It's not just about healing emotional wounds; it's also about recovering the "play muscle!" As adults, we tend to forget how to have fun and be creative because we focus on not failing. But here's the thing: if we don't take chances, we don't learn and are more likely to fail.

Part of inner-child work is asking yourself, "What would you do if you weren't worried about what other people would think?" It's easy to get caught up in what others expect from us, but when we do that, we lose sight of what we really want for ourselves.

And let's not forget that creativity is not just for fun; it's a valuable skill in the workplace. Unfortunately, not many people have time to think through new ideas, but inner-child work can help bring more creativity to your workplace by freeing you from fear and self-consciousness.

And the best part is, when you're free of fear, you become more resilient, able to overcome things that don't go your way, and that, my friend, is true adulting.

Children love everything sparkly, musical, and colorful. We loved coloring, painting, doodling—anything that let our imagination come to reality! Which activity made your eyes light up when you were a kid?

It seemed as though everything was possible. But then we grew up, and that passion and creativity got lost in the world of adulthood along with us. Recalling those days of boundless possibility and the captivating magic of even the simplest toys can bring joy and a sense of nostalgia. The good news is that adopting a childlike attitude can actually lead to significant success, regardless of one's level of creativity.

Studies have demonstrated that spending time in imaginative play has a crucial role in developing the capacity to generate original ideas and in being more imaginative. Research has also found that imagining oneself as a child leads to better results on tests that measure divergent thinking abilities.

So, how can you tap into this childlike creativity? The answer is simple: relax and have fun!

Re-read a Book From Your Childhood

Do you remember your nighttime routine? Your parents tuck you in bed, and you don't let them leave your side until they read you a story. So, they get in bed with you and tell you a story in their calming voice while you slowly drift to sleep. Good times, right?

Kids' books are simple, yet they give way to the imagination like nothing else. *Jack and the Beanstalk, Gulliver's Travels, Rapunzel,* and *Princess and the Pea*—none of them are based on real-life stories, and yet, just by hearing the names of the books, you are taken back in time. You can imagine the fairytales. You can imagine Rapunzel trapped in that tower with her head poking out the window and her long, shiny hair brushing the ground. You can imagine the giant Gulliver making his way through the tiny town with tiny, little people.

Go to your local library and explore the kids' section. Pick up a copy of *Goldilocks and the Three Bears* or *Hansel and Gretel* and immerse yourself in the experience. Treat yourself to fun, easy reads. As soon as you start, your childhood memories will come rushing back to you.

Be Destructive

As adults, we train ourselves to repress our feelings of frustration and anger. How often have you wanted to smash a glass or plate after a tiring day at work? When was the last time you screamed on an empty field? How many years has it been since you punched your pillow?

Allow yourself to feel your emotions. Shred some papers, make scratches on your notebook, and shatter that already broken decoration piece.

Rage rooms and demolition cages are a solution to adult tantrums. It is a safe space that provides glass items such as wine glasses, plates, cups, and ornaments with the purpose of destroying them. The act of smashing and breaking things allows us to de-stress, have fun, and literally shatter our anger.

Make Yourself Laugh

Laughter is like a magic potion that can cure all your troubles! It's like a big ol' dose of happy juice that makes you feel all warm and fuzzy inside. And you know what the best part is? You don't need a prescription for it! All you need to do is let loose, have some fun, and let the laughter flow!

So, want to know the secret to feeling good? Get silly with your kids! Tell knock-knock jokes, play dress-up, and act like a big kid yourself! Put on a video of cat fails from YouTube, a funny movie, or an episode of your favorite sitcom whenever you feel a little down.

Not only will you bond with your little ones, but you'll also reconnect with your inner child who finds joy in everything. It's a win-win situation!

But it's not just fun and games; laughter also has some serious health benefits. It can lower stress levels, boost your immune system, and even improve your heart health! Don't be afraid to let your silly side show; let the laughter flow. It's not just good for the soul; it's good for the body, too!

Recreate Your Childhood

Examine old photo albums to reconnect with your younger self's appearance. Fix this image firmly in your mind, as it will aid your ongoing inner-child work. Consider placing photos of yourself near your bedside, in your wallet, or around your home to continually remind yourself of your inner child's existence.

Take a moment to reflect on what activities brought you joy as a child, such as climbing trees or having warm chocolate milk. Try to incorporate these beloved childhood pastimes into your current life.

"Everything seemed possible when I looked through the eyes of a child.

And every once in a while, I remember,

I still have the chance to be that wild."

- Nikki Rowe

Through inner-child work, many individuals have discovered previously unknown aspects of themselves, leading to profound transformation. Incorporating playtime into your routine is essential for this process. It's normal to feel self-conscious or silly at first, but it is important to approach this exploration with an open and accepting mindset.

Remember your best friend in high school? Do you wonder where they are and how they ended up? It may be time to shoot them a DM or call them up. Ask them how they are doing and about their life since school. It may take you back in time, or who knows? You may revive that friendship again.

Be Open to Learning New Things

Adults often have a more practical, goal-oriented mindset. They tend to focus on problem-solving and getting things done and may be more likely to approach new situations with a sense of caution and a desire to control the outcome. Children, on the other hand, tend to approach the world with a sense of wonder and an openness to learn and explore. They are less concerned with practical outcomes and more interested in simply experiencing the world around them.

To connect with one's inner child, it can be helpful to let go of the constant need to fix and control. Instead, try to approach situations with an open mind and a willingness to learn. This can help you see the learning opportunities present in your everyday life and approach new situations with a sense of curiosity and wonder rather than with a sense of anxiety or control.

Daydream and Visualize

Recall how the world seemed much brighter and more colorful when you were a child. Visualization can help you tap into your senses and imagination. It is crucial to heed the inner voice that encourages creativity and spontaneity. As children, we naturally pursued activities that brought us joy and excitement without overthinking or worrying about the consequences.

As adults, we can tap into this carefree spirit by indulging in activities that bring out our big smiles and infectious laughter. This can mean exploring our hobbies and imagination, staying playful and pursuing our passions, and living in wonder like kids do when they discover the joy in simple things like playing in the rain. By embracing these activities, we can chase after happiness and contentment that is not based on material wealth or power but rather on the pure bliss that comes from within.

Use your senses and view the world from a different perspective. Take your time to appreciate the colors of the walls as you walk by. Take in the smell of freshly made coffee. Feel the texture of the boots you just got. Hear the sound the washing machine makes as it swirls your clothes around.

Sometimes It Plays to Be a Little Wild

Think about it like this: Have you ever noticed how kids have no problem expressing themselves freely, whether it's through silly dances, wild screams, or imaginative play? They don't hold back or censor themselves; they just let it all out. Well, inner child work is kind of like permitting yourself to tap back into that wild, carefree expression.

When you act wild, you're allowing your inner child to come out and play. It's a chance to let loose, get silly, and just have fun! And who doesn't need more of that in their life, right? By letting go and acting wild, you can release any pent-up emotions and stress, allowing yourself to connect with your inner child on a deeper level.

Go dance to that song you like and play "house" with a set of dolls. Go all out on Halloween with roleplaying and a face full of green makeup! Let your imagination show itself in the real world without caring what others might think of you. Allowing the body to move freely and expressively can help to release stored emotions and connect with the inner child, while playing with toys evokes a sense of playfulness and innocence.

So, whether you're twirling around like a ballerina, jumping up and down like a kangaroo, or making silly faces in the mirror, just remember: you're not just acting wild; you're also healing your inner child.

Shake Things Up

We live a routine: get up, eat, go to work, and sleep. Nothing takes the magic away of being present more than this monotonous routine. Sure, you need to be organized and disciplined to have your life in order, but we should not get lost in it. Appreciating the little things in our lives and cherishing the good moments is important. We need to perceive reality without its notions and patterns. It is time we push these patterns aside.

While patterns are helpful in understanding the world, it's important to periodically step back and experience the present moment without categorizing or labeling it. This helps us recognize that much of what we take for granted in our daily lives is just an illusion. To practice this, one can take a brief moment in their day to simply be present and observe their surroundings without categorizing. It is important that we introduce new things in our lives. It may be a new book, a new milkshake, a new cup, or anything! You can just change the shower drapes, and you will feel different.

Write to Yourself

You can also use writing to communicate with your inner child. For example, you can write a letter to your inner child, addressing any issues or concerns that you may have. This can be a powerful way to express your feelings and validate and support your inner child.

Think about everything you wish you could have told yourself back in the day. Maybe you needed a little extra support or a reminder to be kind to yourself. Whatever it is, now's the time to send that message. By reconnecting with your inner child through writing, you can start to heal old wounds and feel more at peace with the past. Plus, it's a great way to strengthen that bond with your younger self and give them the love and guidance they need.

An example:

Dear Inner Child, let's have a heart-to-heart! Today wasn't the easiest day for me; I disagreed with someone close to me, leaving me feeling upset and on edge. But as I sit down and write to you, I am reminded of all our love and support for each other. You bring back fond memories of the new friendships I made after a difficult time and give me the bravery to express my emotions.

You are my rock, my comfort, and every time I talk to you through my daily journal, I feel our connection growing stronger and our healing journey becoming clearer. From the fun summer days spent playing outside to the comforting nights spent snuggled up with a good book, you have been there for me through it all.

Thank you for being such an important part of my life, inner child. I promise to continue to listen to you and care for you every step of the way. I love you now and always and give you a big, comforting hug.

Journal Your Way In

One way to reconnect with your inner child is through journaling. This can be a fun and creative way to explore your feelings and memories. Try writing a letter to your inner child, letting them know you're here for them and want to listen to what they say. You can also journal about your childhood experiences and any emotions that come up.

When journaling and thinking back to childhood memories, it is important to focus on the specific details of the memory. This includes the location, the people present during it, and the emotions that were felt. By doing this, you can gain a deeper understanding of the memory and the emotions that were associated with it. It is possible that by reflecting on these memories, you may uncover emotions you were unaware of at the time of the memory.

This can help provide insight into how these emotions may impact your current thoughts and behaviors. Reflecting on childhood memories in a journal can help to gain a deeper understanding of these memories, emotions, and how they may be impacting your current thoughts and behaviors.

Listen to yourself

So, you know when you're having a rough day, and everything just seems to be getting on your nerves? Like, the barista spelled your name wrong on your latte, or your boss does not understand that you need a break? Well, it's important to pay attention to these triggers and determine where they're coming from. It's like a mystery, but instead of a physical crime, it's emotional.

And who are you talking to when these emotions are popping up? Are you talking to your bestie, your partner, or maybe even yourself? It's important to keep an eye on these interactions because they might be connected to some childhood stuff that you haven't dealt with yet.

But don't worry; there's hope! By practicing self-care and caring for your needs, you're showing yourself some much-needed love. It's like hugging yourself from the inside out. Trust me, it's a powerful act of self-love, and it can help you heal those old wounds.

Build a new set of caregivers

Let's talk about our parents. Now, I know they're not perfect, and neither are we, but as we grow up, we start to realize just how much they didn't know when they were raising us. And even if they did the best they could, sometimes we still hold a bit of resentment towards them.

But here's the thing: you can't go back in time and change the past, but you can control how you react to it right now. It's like being your own parent, and when you feel your inner child getting upset, you step in and take care of yourself the way you wish someone would have when you were young.

Self-care and compassion are key. Instead of dwelling on past mistakes, focus on caring for yourself in the present moment. It's a powerful way to heal and move forward.

Talk to your loved ones

Many individuals hold grudges against family members or individuals from their childhood who have hurt them. These grudges may manifest as blame towards these individuals for shaping who they are today, or they may vow to be nothing like them. However, as children, we were likely disconnected from the challenges and struggles that these individuals may have been facing as adults.

Recently, I had a conversation with a family member whom I love but had always perceived as mean. This individual was in their forties when I was born, so it had always seemed like we had little in common. However, during this conversation, I was able to hear stories about their childhood and early adulthood. For the first time, I began to understand the difficult experiences they had faced. This understanding gave me a more compassionate and empathetic perspective toward them.

It is important to note that someone else's struggles do not excuse any form of abuse. However, understanding their perspective and seeing your interactions with them from a different angle can provide closure and help build or repair relationships with individuals you had previously written off.

Therapy

Inner-child therapy focuses on helping individuals understand and address the emotional wounds and experiences from their childhood that may still be impacting them in their adult lives. This type of therapy is offered by mental health professionals who specialize in it and may use various techniques such as shadow work, attachment theory, psychoanalysis, and art therapy.

The therapist will help the client identify specific memories and triggers that still affect them and how they are connected to their childhood experiences. This process can help individuals understand and process their past experiences to improve their emotional well-being and relationships in the present.

But Why?

As parents, we've all been there; the constant bombardment of "why" from our curious little ones can drive us up the wall. But behind the annoyance lies a powerful force—a deep and insatiable curiosity about the world around us. So, why have we as adults stopped asking "why?"

I believe it's important for us to keep asking questions, to keep that wild curiosity alive. By doing so, we can continue to learn about ourselves, others, and the world around us. The truth is, there's so much out there that we don't know and even more that we don't realize we don't know. But by asking questions, we open ourselves up to the possibility of discovering great treasures, embarking on exciting adventures, and finding beautiful and simple solutions to problems we thought were set in stone. Do not give up on your curiosity—keep asking "why" and see where it takes you!

Never Give Up Your Playtime

Growing up can be a bummer sometimes because we must say goodbye to all the fun and games. It's like, "Bye-bye, childhood; hello, adulting!" We start to think that we have to be super serious all the time and that being silly is for kids. But the truth is, being serious all the time is like eating broccoli for breakfast, lunch, and dinner. It's just not fun!

Growing up has its perks, but losing touch with one's inner child is not one of them. Embrace the fun and simple activities to bring back the joy and simplicity of childhood and see how life becomes more beautiful.

"My childhood may be over, but that doesn't mean playtime is."

- Ron Olson

We also start to stress about making mistakes and fail to realize that making mistakes is just a part of life. It's like getting a "game over" in a video game; you just gotta hit the restart button and try again. But instead, we let the fear of failure control us and make us feel like we're stuck in a never-ending game of Simon Says. Do not forget to have some fun and play along the way because if we don't, life will be as boring as watching paint dry! And who wants that?

Recreate Your Childhood

Remember how you used to spend your weekends as a kid? Whether riding bikes, collecting stamps, or making art, those hobbies were a big part of your childhood. Why not pick one of those hobbies back up as an adult? You'll be able to tap into that inner child and relive some of your fondest memories.

Why settle for a dull coffee catch-up when you can have a night of wild fun with your besties? Forget about adulting for a night and let loose with a sleepover filled with snacks, pillow forts, movie marathons, and endless chats. Not only will you relive your teenage years, but you'll also make memories that will bring you even closer to your friends. And let's be real, who doesn't love a good slumber party?

Crank up your favorite tunes and let loose like nobody's watching (cause let's face it, nobody is)! Dancing is an amazing way to connect with your body and shake off any jitters. But most importantly, it's just plain old fun.

Play With Your Loved Ones!

As a child, playtime was an integral part of your day and was cherished and enjoyed to the fullest. After school, you would gather with friends, engage in fun activities, play with toys, or watch TV. This time was a source of happiness and the highlight of the day.

However, as you grow older, life becomes more demanding, and finding time to rest becomes challenging. This can lead to feelings of boredom, fatigue, and procrastination. Setting aside time for activities that bring joy and happiness, reminiscent of your childhood playtime, is important to overcome this. Don't let anything or anyone take this away from you, as regularly engaging in play can rekindle the connection with your inner child.

Engaging in playful activities with loved ones can help alleviate stress and make you more fun and enjoyable to be around. It suggests that constantly carrying stress can be tiring and that it is important to take a break from being serious and engage in activities that bring joy and playfulness. This can be done by spending quality time with family and loved ones, such as playing with your kids or engaging in fun activities with your partner. Allowing yourself to let go of stress and be more playful can help improve your mood and overall well-being.

Communicate!

Communicating with your inner child can be difficult, as the messages and clues it sends may be easily overlooked amid a busy daily life. To effectively communicate with your inner child, setting aside dedicated time for self-discovery and reflection is important. This can be achieved through various practices such as meditation or journaling.

One specific method that can be used is a visualization exercise in which you sit in a quiet, comfortable room and close your eyes. Imagine yourself as a child, around the age at which you suspect any past trauma occurred. Allow this inner child to express their feelings and emotions, whether it be through crying, yelling, or other forms of expression. Including specific details and people connected to the trauma can be helpful, such as parents.

For example, you can use art therapy to express yourself through drawing, painting, or even sculpting. You can also use music therapy, where you can sing or play an instrument, as a way to connect with your inner child. This can help tap into emotions and memories that may be difficult to access through other forms of communication.

Once you have a clear visualization of your child self, you can ask questions such as:

- What does the child want from life?

- How are they doing?

- Why do they not display their emotions?

- Why do they have trouble asking for help?

- What are they blaming themselves for?

- What can you say to make them feel secure?

You do not have to ask all these questions at once; even one question can make a difference and show the inner child that someone cares. This exercise can be done with a therapist or on your own, but it is important to have a quiet, comfortable space and fully engage with the visualization.

It's important to note that there is no specific way to communicate with your inner child, and different methods may work better for different people. The most important thing is to find a method that resonates with you and consistently practice it.

Look For the Patterns

It is common to repeat familiar patterns, even if they bring discomfort or dissatisfaction. For example, individuals with abandonment issues stemming from childhood may find themselves repeatedly choosing personal or professional relationships where there is a high likelihood of being left behind. Additionally, they may unconsciously push away people who could bring positivity into their lives out of fear of abandonment.

Recognizing and acknowledging these negative patterns that stem from childhood can help to bring about change and promote healthier behaviors. Everyone has unhealthy patterns from childhood that they recreate in adulthood, so it is important to be gentle and forgiving with oneself upon discovery.

The Love Hormone

Oxytocin is a hormone produced in response to feelings of love and safety. It has numerous benefits, including reducing stress, boosting immunity, and promoting sleep, relaxation, and positive thinking. However, neglect from a caregiver during childhood can inhibit the release of oxytocin and other hormones like dopamine.

Studies reveal that oxytocin is produced in the hypothalamus and can be released into the bloodstream to aid in uterine contractions and milk production. It also directly impacts the brain and plays a crucial role in forming and maintaining attachment bonds in animals.

Fortunately, there are ways to stimulate the release of oxytocin in adulthood, and some studies are exploring administering oxytocin to children to foster trust and safety.

Ways to release oxytocin as an adult include:

1. Massage, either self-massage or from a partner.

2. Taking a relaxing bath with warm water and bubbles.

3. Listening to or making music.

4. Practicing yoga lowers blood pressure and reduces

stress.

5. Physical intimacy, such as hugging, cuddling, or sex.

6. Building a supportive network and engaging in social activities.

7. Using a weighted blanket for a comforting hug.

8. Meditating, such as the "Inner Child Healing Meditation" on YouTube.

9. Interacting with animals, whether through petting or getting an emotional support pet.

Say It Out Loud

To provide emotional healing to your inner child, consider selecting some affirming statements they may need to hear. Write these affirmations on a post-it note and place it in a prominent location in your room. Each morning, take a moment to read these affirmations out loud to your inner child, speaking directly to them and allowing them to internalize the message.

Here are some examples to get you started:

- "I deeply love and accept you just as you are."

- "I'm sorry for any pain or hurt that you may have experienced in the past."

- "You have complete control over your body and the choices you make regarding it."

- "You have the right to explore, have fun, and be curious in this world."

- "Your body is a safe and loving place for you to reside in."

Set Boundaries and Practice Self-Care

The phrase "loving discipline" refers to the act of setting and adhering to personal boundaries. This involves being kind and understanding with oneself when mistakes are made and taking responsibility for correcting them. Additionally, it involves being faithful to oneself by keeping promises and prioritizing one's own needs. By consistently practicing loving discipline, especially when starting new habits, one can develop greater self-confidence and self-reliance.

To improve your overall well-being, it is important to understand your deep-seated emotional needs, particularly those not fulfilled during childhood. Once you have identified these needs, you can actively work towards satisfying them through various self-care activities that support your physical, mental, and spiritual health.

Self-care is all about taking care of yourself and protecting your well-being, and there are many ways to do this. For instance, keeping a journal, practicing meditation, drinking enough water, eating nutritious food, taking breaks to rest, asking for assistance when needed, and nurturing positive relationships with others are all excellent self-care practices that can help you feel rejuvenated, refreshed, and reinvigorated.

Emotional Deep Dive

It is a universal truth that everyone has some form of childhood wound, regardless of whether their childhood was ideal, difficult, or somewhere in between. When reflecting on their childhood, many individuals may long for elements lacking in their upbringing, such as increased affection, unconditional love, fun-loving adults, safety, a sense of belonging, stability, resources, support, independence, validation, recognition, or other forms of support. The reality is that no one's childhood was flawless, and for some individuals, their childhood experiences were incredibly distressing.

"The process of reclaiming your wounded inner child is a forgiveness process. Forgiveness allows us to give as before. It heals the past and frees our energies for the present."

- John Bradshaw

Be the Change You Wanted

One of the challenges of childhood is the dependence on others for various aspects of life. If financial stability was a concern during childhood, it is important to create more financial security in adulthood. For individuals who felt invisible during childhood, it is crucial to prioritize self-care and attend to their own needs and wants. Building relationships with people who acknowledge and appreciate their uniqueness can help foster a sense of self-worth and fulfillment. These individuals should surround themselves with individuals who see them as special and value their presence.

Do Your Part

If you experienced a traumatic childhood, it's normal to feel triggered or even experience feelings of envy when encountering children or teenagers with seemingly perfect childhoods. It's important to remind yourself that all children require love and affection, regardless of their upbringing.

You have the opportunity to be a positive influence in the life of a child, whether they are your own, a relative's, a friend's, a student, or someone you meet through volunteer work. Show them affection and make them feel special. You will likely have opportunities to make a difference in their lives, whether in small or significant ways. Make a conscious and dedicated effort to be a caring and supportive figure in a child's life in your surroundings. This will bring healing and growth to both you and the child.

Try New Things

Traveling to new places and trying new things is a great way to feel more connected with the inner child. Find a destination that excites you and brings you joy, and then go all in! Whether trying a new cuisine, meeting new people, or even tackling an adventure sport, the idea is to do something you've never done before.

By doing these things, you'll be taken back to a time when you didn't have to worry about the outcome; you just did what made you happy. And once you understand how to find happiness by following your heart, it'll be much easier to connect with your inner child and keep that feeling going.

Don't Be Afraid to Take Chances

As adults, we often become cautious and hesitant to take risks. We tend to overthink and underact, content with staying within our comfort zones. However, when we were children, we were much different. We didn't allow ourselves to become trapped or limited. Instead, we were constantly learning, adapting, and growing. We pushed the boundaries of our limitations.

To rediscover your inner child, you need to break out of this comfort zone and embrace all the amazing opportunities the world has to offer. Your inner child desires adventure and change. It longs for you to explore new experiences and keep growing.

CHAPTER 6: THE ROLE OF SELF-ESTEEM IN OUR INNER CHILD

Many individuals have an inner child within them who embodies their youthful energy, curiosity, and optimism. However, this inner child also experiences fear, pain, and insecurity. This inner child is often imagined in a dark corner, cowering and protecting itself from internal voices that judge and attack them.

These voices may criticize the inner child for not meeting society's expectations, being too passive, or lacking morality. This self-criticism and internal judgment can damage a person's confidence and negatively impact their aspirations. The inner child's experiences significantly impact a person's outer self, affecting their sense of self-worth and ability to pursue their goals.

Our self-image, self-respect, and self-esteem play a crucial role in shaping our life decisions. Humans appear to be on a never-ending quest for happiness, expressed through choices regarding love, work, and relationships and influenced by our values and experiences.

Confidence plays a significant role in helping individuals pursue their aspirations and take risks. Those with a higher level of confidence often have an inner child nurtured and comforted by positive internal voices. These voices provide support, encouragement, and comfort to the inner child, helping them to feel valued and worthy.

"The internal war you wage with yourself may not be seen by others but is always felt by you!"

- Lorraine Nilon

These internal voices often result from the messages received during childhood from caregivers and important figures in our lives. At a young age, our brains absorb information, and we believe what we are told about ourselves, including messages that can be harmful and limiting. These negative messages can be internalized and become constant sources of self-doubt and insecurity.

Our inner child, guided by our internal thoughts and beliefs, shapes how we view ourselves and the world. If these voices are critical or negative, it can lead to a self-critical view and a belief that one does not deserve love or nurturing. As a result, relationships can become difficult or even impossible. We may look for partners who mirror our own self-disrespect, seeking approval from others and being submissive to win their approval. Our self-doubt can hold us back from pursuing opportunities or careers that align with our passions.

"The child wants simple things. It wants to be listened to. It wants to be loved.... It may not even know the words, but it wants its rights protected and its self-respect unviolated. It needs you to be there."

- Ron Kurz

However, it is possible to heal the inner child's wounds by transforming these negative thoughts and voices into positive, nurturing ones. This can be achieved with patience and effort through therapy, self-reflection, or mindfulness practices. By doing so, individuals can break free from the limiting beliefs and pain that hold them back and lead a more fulfilling life.

Inner Child and Karma

The concept of karma states that our unfulfilled desires from past lives drive our current existence. This cycle also occurs in each moment as unconscious, unmet needs shape our actions. The inner child, representing past traumas, yearns for healing and can either retreat or lash out in response to intense emotions like fear, anger, shame, or guilt. This inner child often relies on rigid thinking patterns and beliefs to protect itself. It requires love and guidance from the adult self to build trust and feel complete.

Until the inner child is healed, past struggles will persist. The cycle of repetition can only be broken through conscious effort. Eastern philosophy recognizes the influence of karma as stored subconscious seeds that impact our lives until they are transformed through self-awareness or replaced with positive ones. Fortunately, the forces of the inner child can also be redeemed and bring positive outcomes through the cultivation of positive karma.

As individuals, it is essential that we nurture our inner child and give them the love, support, and care they deserve. We must tell them that they are good and loved just as they are, no matter what. When mistakes happen, we must remind them that it is okay and that they can learn and do better next time. When fear and anxiety take hold, we must be there to hold their hand, to soothe and reassure them that they are strong and capable. And when we feel exhausted, we must offer encouragement and push them to keep going, to never give up on their dreams.

"I want you to imagine what you would do if you had come upon that real child in the original situation... What's a reasonable, compassionate thing to do for a child that's confused and upset? You sit and talk with the child. You listen to it. You find out what's bothering it, help it understand, comfort it, hold it in your arms; later, you play with it a little, explain things, and tell a story. That's therapy in its oldest and best sense: nothing fancy, just kindness and patience."

- Ron Kurz

Through this self-parenting, our inner child will gain the confidence and self-assurance to stand tall and face the world. They will no longer be afraid of the judgment and criticism of others, and instead, they will reach for the stars and chase their dreams with unwavering determination. By nurturing and loving our inner child, we give them the voice they need to live a fulfilling life with self-belief and hope.

"I Hate Myself"

The world is full of sad people and trauma, and it all starts with their childhood. The tiny humans arrive in the world completely at the mercy of other human beings. They do not have any say of their own, any strength, or any support; they depend solely on their caregivers for care and love.

However, things can get a little fuzzy if the promised love isn't provided to them. The child starts yearning for love and goes all the way to get even a little bit of it. The child will start to try a lot harder to "charm" their parents, to be good, to get a smile out of them, or even just a word of appreciation.

People who grow up in a non-supportive or loveless environment tend to undermine themselves, their abilities, and their strengths. They do not know how to care for themselves or love themselves because no one ever showed them how. They spend their life thinking that they are so unlovable that the ones who were supposed to give them unconditional love did not even like them. They start hating themselves instead of questioning those who failed to protect and nurture them. They start feeling helpless, holding themselves to unrealistic standards and false blames. And so the cycle of self-hatred starts. They grow up mentally disturbed, unhappy, and unable to really make their life fruitful.

They do not believe they deserve love or "nice things." They grow up sabotaging their every move, unable to progress in life. They get into a cycle of depression, taking comfort in drugs, alcohol, and other activities such as gaming or food. They never allow themselves to be truly happy and spend their lives on the sidelines, being the "wallflower." Often, suicidal thoughts creep into their minds, and they subconsciously start living just to survive, not enjoy life. They distance themselves from people who care about them because they are not used to being cared for.

"Not Good Enough"

Childhood is a time when many individuals can start feeling inadequate and inferior due to unfair treatment and mistreatment. The tone of voice that your parents used with you subconsciously becomes the voice of your inner child. Even if their intentions were good, they imprint things in their minds to last forever, ultimately costing us a life of negative thoughts.

What does your inner voice say to you? Does it still echo the careless tone of your math teacher saying, "You will fail?" Does it still remind you of when your overbearing mother said in an hour of emotion, "You are a disgrace to this family," or when your overachieving father said as a joke, "That kid tops every class; why can't you be more like him?" There's that sluggish remark from your sibling on your weight, "How will you get someone to love you with all the weight you have put on," and the comment of the mean girl in your class that said, "Ew, your face acne is so gross?"

The person you loved wholeheartedly made fun of your insecurity, saying, "You are so short!" You see magazines and movies and always come down with the blues, thinking that you will never achieve what they have or that you will never be as pretty or handsome as they are because your family and friends subconsciously made you believe as such.

And it is not totally out of the blue that you feel this way. The people around you are supposed to lift you up, not crush you. What they always say matters to you, and you start thinking about yourself the same way that they judge you. You may feel that you are never enough due to unrealistic standards, comparison with others, and being made to feel worthless. This toxic mindset can lead to constant self-doubt, never feeling like your actions are good enough, an overwhelming need to do more, and an inability to relax and just be. It's a painful and damaging cycle that can last a lifetime.

"Alone and Unloved"

Parents are supposed to cater to their kids, help them, support them, and love them so they can grow up to be their best selves. However, sometimes, parents think of their children as their saviors, born to care for them, give them love, help them, and make their needs come true. Such elders see their children as their slaves, their pets, and their property that they can use however they want. And so, some children grow up to be exactly that, as failing to do so often resulted in punishment, abuse, shame, and guilt. They undermine their own wishes and happiness to pursue others. They are what we call "the parent of the group," always taking care of others and putting their own needs out of the picture.

This child, who was supposed to be nurtured and assisted, learns to sacrifice himself for others his whole life. These people pleasers tend to ignore self-care and become detached from themselves in the long haul. This leads to a life full of emotional confusion and an inability to defend themselves from the cruelty of life.

Several such people who tend to "live for others" have different beliefs. They enjoy giving to people and pleasing others; however, they expect something in return and get confused when people do not behave as they want them to. They believe they are the good in the world and do not do well with negative treatment. They do not understand why people do not "give back" when they are so "nice and caring" towards them.

"I've promised my inner child that never again will I ever abandon myself for anyone else again."

- Wynonna Judd

"I Feel No Pain"

It is important to note that a poor childhood does not always result in self-loathing and hatred. Early experiences and trauma show up in many personality disorders, including narcissism. Such people grow up under the umbrella of narcissistic parents or other relatives who abuse them emotionally or physically. And they want only one thing from the world: revenge.

They believe they must not show emotion to the world as it is a sign of weakness and stupidity. They shove every feeling deep inside so they can confidently face the world. This fake confidence makes them appear happy and secure to anyone they interact with. They don't blame their abuse on their caregivers as they believe to be supporting their cause.

They look for things and people to fulfill their needs and their empty hearts with love. They put on a happy face to lure people in, and once they are trapped, they take out their abuse and trauma on them because they believe it to be the norm. The abuse starts so small that you do not even notice it. You often just get confused and feel guilty for your "oopsies." It starts with a public joke at your expense, and then it slowly gets to the point where you see no way out.

"Narcissists are consumed with maintaining a shallow false self to others. They're emotionally crippled souls that are addicted to attention. Because of this, they use a multitude of games, in order to receive adoration. Sadly, they are the most ungodly of God's creations because they don't show remorse for their actions, take steps to make amends, or have empathy for others. They are morally bankrupt."

- Shannon L. Alder

These sadists feel no remorse for their actions, so they never understand the complaints and anger. Once their loveless void is filled, their real self emerges, and they believe you are the cause of all their problems and that they must make you suffer. They live a secret life, appearing as someone else to friends and someone else to their family.

"I Am Better Than Everyone"

A narcissistic personality is not just the result of a bad up-bringing and "crazy" families. There are supporting families, and then there are families that put high pressure on you to be the best you can be. They want to fulfill their dreams and desires through you, so they constantly push you to meet their needs. Such narcissistic parents do not necessarily hit you or abuse you in any way, but they also do not believe your life to be your own.

They believe you to be born for a purpose, and they control your life, picking and choosing everything for you. They do not let you live your own way and mold you to become another version of themselves while making you believe that they are doing everything in your best interest and for your betterment only.

People who grow up in such an environment face a hard time going out in the "real world." Such personalities believe in having the upper hand in everything and believe they are superior and better than anyone. They are so used to being appreciated and cheered for everything that they get confused when they are not met with the same "supportive" audience elsewhere. They always believed they were unique, special, and one of a kind, and now no one else is saying these things to them. They start questioning everything in life. "If I am so great, why am I alone? Why do I not have any friends?" They influence all their relationships and push people away with their self-perception. They believe they should be treated a certain way just because they are, well, them.

'I Am a Victim'

This type of narcissist lives their whole life as a "victim." They received bad treatment in childhood in the form of neglect, abuse, and maltreatment, and they believe that other people should fill the gaps. They keep waiting for people to come around and fulfill their desires and needs, giving them the life they were deprived of. They keep waving their mantra in people's faces: "I am the one who was abused physically and emotionally, not you. I deserve the special treatment. I deserve all the love I wasn't given." Contrary to what we discussed above, this type of personality always puts their desires before others.

They believe they can skate through life waving the "I am a victim" flag. They make it their whole identity and keep getting themselves in abusive situations. They believe that the world is out to get them and that everything bad is in their destiny and must happen to them only. They tend to be attracted to abusive relationships and depend on others for validation and feeling valued. This perception of life costs them their future relationships. People call them "needy," "selfish," or "all in their head."

You Inner Child Is Hurt

As adults, we often deceive ourselves into thinking we've left our childhoods behind. But the reality is that many of us carry a wounded inner child within us, buried deep within our subconscious, desperate for attention and healing.

The truth is that your inner child holds the key to pure joy, unbridled creativity, and true freedom. To unlock this hidden treasure, you must journey within and become a loving parent to the wounded child. Your inner child needs you to confront and process its past traumas, to heal and finally be free to play and enjoy life once again.

The degree of childhood trauma is different for each of us. Some may have faced severe abuse, while others may have experienced subtler forms of neglect, abandonment, or social rejection. Regardless of the specifics, every one of us was once a child, and that child still exists within us today.

Many inner children hide away, waiting for someone to come and acknowledge their pain. They want to express themselves and be carefree and light, but first, they must feel safe and loved. When they can't, it's often due to unresolved childhood traumas that we've learned to suppress and ignore.

Your inner child may sabotage your adult experience by trying to get you to heal its unresolved issues. You can do that by becoming your own parent, providing a loving presence and the self-compassion you wished you had received as a child.

When a parent fails to acknowledge your emotions and make you feel valued, it can deeply impact how you view yourself. Growing up without learning to trust your own feelings can leave you without a strong sense of self-worth, leading you to seek validation from others constantly.

The sad reality is that you may go through life without even realizing the importance of nurturing your emotions. Without self-esteem, you may habitually put your feelings aside to appease others.

It's a heartbreaking cycle where you constantly look to the outside world for the love, acceptance, and validation that should come from within. It often takes hitting rock bottom and feeling lost before you finally begin to turn inward and prioritize your own emotions.

It's a painful cycle that is all too familiar to those who have suffered from inner child wounds. The good news is that it is possible to heal and move past these feelings of insecurity and isolation with time, support, and self-reflection.

It's important to remember that healing and inner child work is not a one-time process; it's a continuous journey. It's about being patient and compassionate with yourself and giving yourself the time and space to heal and grow.

PART 3: HEALING THE WOUNDED INNER CHILD

CHAPTER 7: HOW CAN WE HEAL A WOUNDED INNER CHILD?

"Your ego is a mask that your inner child wears. Underneath it all, your inner child is a costume of innocence decorating the highest self of all. This is the play of existence. The purpose is not to escape the play, but to learn how to play at full capacity for the well-being of all. This is the heart of realization."

- Matt Kahn

As a child, were you filled with joy and delight, surrounded by unconditional love and a sense of safety that made you feel secure in the world? Or, have your childhood memories been buried deep within you, overshadowed by the pain and trauma you endured?

Childhood adversities often leave a lasting impact on individuals, leading them to develop various psychological defense mechanisms and survival strategies. Some become overly submissive, sacrificing their own needs and desires to please others, while others become extremely self-absorbed, using others for their own gain. Some struggle to find peace and relaxation, constantly feeling the need to do more, while others feel trapped in a victim mentality, living a passive life. Despite their best efforts, a nagging feeling of inadequacy and unhappiness persists, causing them to question their worth and search for something more fulfilling.

Breaking free from the past is not easy, but it can bring a sense of freedom and liberation that is unmatched. The reward for those who try to heal from their childhood adversity is a life filled with authenticity and joy, making all the hard work worth it.

Do you remember being a child and feeling safe, loved, and carefree? As we grow and mature, we often forget what it feels like to be that innocent, vulnerable child. But deep within us, there's a part of us that never really grows up, a part that holds onto the memories, emotions, and experiences of our childhood. This part of us is often called the "kid within."

Although the kid within may not have a physical form, its presence can be felt in how we interact with the world and our choices. Our past experiences and emotions shape how we perceive ourselves and others and can influence our relationships, career choices, and mental health.

Unfortunately, many of us have experienced childhood trauma that can leave deep wounds that never fully heal. Childhood trauma can take many different forms, including, but not limited to, abuse, neglect, bullying, natural disasters, financial distress, car accidents, family substance use disorders, domestic violence, being a refugee, and more. These traumatic experiences can leave a lasting impact on our sense of safety, security, and well-being.

It's important to acknowledge the reality of our childhood experiences and understand their role in shaping who we are as adults. With understanding comes the possibility of healing and moving forward in a more positive, fulfilling direction.

It can be overwhelming to confront the inner demons of fear, trauma, and pain that run so much deeper than the current events in our lives. The cries of our inner child for love, acceptance, and comfort can feel deafening, leaving us lost and unsure of where to turn.

But it's noteworthy to remember that healing is possible. The journey to overcoming the wounds that have cost us our innocence may seem daunting, but it's a necessary step in reclaiming the life we deserve.

We try to escape the wounds of our past, hiding from the pain and suffering that we believe we can't bear. But the hurt child within us is relentless, constantly begging for our attention and trying to break through the walls we've built. Our fear of the pain takes hold, and we turn to distractions, but they only offer fleeting solace, leaving the wound unhealed and festering.

Ignorance is our enemy, clouding our vision and leading us down paths of self-destruction, perpetuating the cycle of suffering. But the power to heal also lies within us, passed down from generations before us. We have the capability to ignite the flame of mindfulness and tap into the wisdom and love that rests within us. Mindfulness is the key, the foundation upon which we build our path to healing.

Through our mindful breaths, steps, and peaceful smile, we can cultivate the energy of mindfulness and embrace the wounded child within us, bringing peace and solace to the pain of our past.

Once we acknowledge the forgotten child within, we can tap into the power of mindfulness through walking, sitting, and breathing. This power will heal and embrace us, reinvigorating the wisdom and calm in every cell of our body and healing the wounded child within.

"Things your inner child might need to hear: It's not your fault when other people are in bad moods. You are worthy of everything good. It's okay to feel. You are not alone; I am with you. You are a good person and I love you. You are worth protecting. You are beautiful and loved. What happened to you was not your fault."

How To Reconnect With the Trapped Child Inside

First, it's important to understand that our "inner child" is the part of us that holds all of our emotional memories and experiences from childhood. As we grow up and navigate the adult world, it's easy for our inner child to get "trapped" and not fully express themselves. But don't worry; there are ways to reconnect with this part of yourself and set it free!

"The wound is not my fault. But the healing is my responsibility."

- Marianne Williamson

Exercise 1. Talk to the Mini You

When fear and anxiety start to take hold of you, take a moment to connect with your inner child. Close your eyes and imagine her there, small and vulnerable, and reach out to her with a gentle embrace. Speak to her in a voice filled with passion and conviction, and tell her that she is strong, loved, and will weather this storm. Let the power of your words wash over her, and watch as her worries slowly melt away. Know that as you speak to her, you are speaking to yourself, reminding yourself of your own strength and resilience. Take a deep breath, and let the sound of your voice fill the room with hope and courage. You'll be astounded at how speaking aloud to yourself can transform your fears into confidence and your worries into peace.

Hey, there, younger self!

Wow, look at you, all grown up and stuff! I bet you're wondering what the future holds, huh? Well, let me tell you, it's pretty amazing. But before I get into all the cool things that are yet to come, I want to take a moment to talk to you about the things that have happened in the past.

I know you've been through some tough times, and it can be hard to move past them. But I want you to know that you are strong and will get through this. You're going to have to be brave, and you're going to have to fight, but you can do it. You are capable of so much more than you think you are.

I also want to remind you to be kind to yourself. You are your own worst critic, and you need to stop being so hard on yourself. You are doing the best you can with what you have, and that is more than enough.

Now, let's talk about the future. You're going to go on some amazing adventures, meet some incredible people, and do some truly amazing things. You'll make mistakes, but that's okay because that's how we learn and grow. You're going to fall in love, and it will be the most beautiful thing you've ever experienced.

And even though there will be tough times ahead, just remember you are capable of overcoming them. You are strong, you are brave, and you are loved.

So, take a deep breath, hold your head high, and keep moving forward. I'll be cheering you on every step of the way.

Love,

Your older self.

Exercise 2. Let The Stress Fade Away

Growing up, you experienced a lack of love, care, and attention that every child deserves to receive. As a result, you sought validation and comfort from the outside world, relying on others to fill the void within you. But now, as an adult, you have the power to heal those wounds and nurture yourself from the inside out.

Dedicating time each week to taking care of yourself and your emotional well-being is important. This can be as simple as taking a walk on the wet grass while barefoot, spending a creative evening in the company of your arts and crafts supplies, bringing out the old DIY tips and tricks, or, my favorite, just dancing around the house like nobody's watching. Try to engage in activities that you enjoyed as a child, such as coloring, playing with clay, or going on a journey in beautiful nature. These activities can awaken the joy and spirit of your inner child, reminding you of the importance of self-care.

Neglecting yourself can lead to an unfulfilling life and inauthentic relationships with others and your work. By prioritizing self-care and self-nurturance, you can create a sense of balance and fulfillment that will positively impact all aspects of your life. Don't be afraid to show yourself love and compassion. You deserve to feel happy, healthy, and fulfilled.

Exercise 3. Let Your Imagination Take Over

The wounds of your inner child can leave a deep impact on your subconscious, manifesting as heavy and dark energy that clouds your thoughts and emotions. But there is hope! By harnessing the power of your imagination, you can begin to release this burdensome energy and reclaim your sense of joy and inner peace.

Take a few minutes each day to imagine yourself as a young, carefree child. Picture yourself playing in a sun-drenched park with the wind in your hair and a smile on your face as you pass the ball to your parents or siblings and scream, "I win!" Maybe you see yourself playing with your favorite pet, feeling the unconditional love and joy that animals bring. Or imagine yourself on a sandy beach, feeling the warmth of the sun and the cool water on your feet without caring about how messy the mud is making you. Or perhaps you picture yourself surrounded by your favorite car or doll collection, lost in the wonder and excitement of your latest score.

Let your imagination take over in every way; become the child completely. See yourself filled with a sense of fun, safety, and love. This is your chance to reclaim your inner joy and let go of the negative energies of the past. By doing this every day, you can tap into the childlike wonder that once lived within you and bring a renewed sense of hope and happiness into your life.

Exercise 4. Be a Good Listener

The practice of listening with compassion involves not just listening to others but also to the hurt child within us. This inner child often calls for attention, and it is important to be mindful and hear its voice.

To heal this wound, we must embrace and talk to this child with love and understanding, saying things like "I am here for you," "I will take care of you," and "I know you are suffering." It is necessary to cry and sit with this child, breathing and comforting them. Healing can only take place if we regularly take the time to connect with this inner child and engage in daily conversation and affectionate gestures. This could be as simple as enjoying a childhood meal or walking together to enjoy the beautiful sunset.

This practice benefits not only ourselves but also our ancestors and descendants who may have passed down the wounded child. By healing this inner child, we free ourselves and help those who may have hurt us, as they may also have been abuse victims. We can reduce suffering, restore relationships, and bring peace and love into our lives with mindfulness, compassion, and understanding.

It's essential that we return to ourselves to be present and mindful in everything we do. Our body, mind, and spirit all require our attention and care, and our wounded inner child is no exception. We must also be mindful of the wounded children in those around us and help them. By embracing our feelings and acknowledging our suffering, we can make a positive impact on our lives and the lives of those we love.

Exercise 5. Back To the Past

Dealing with past emotions and traumatic memories can be incredibly hard. However, exploring your childhood experiences can be a powerful tool in understanding and healing from these difficulties. Use the Childhood Timeline worksheet to map out key events from your birth to 21 years old and uncover any patterns or experiences that may have contributed to challenges later in life.

Dive into your childhood memories and relive your younger self's feelings. Take a trip down memory lane and try to recall the emotions, experiences, and the sense of safety, support, and acceptance you felt during each stage. Remember, the feeling of safety wasn't always just about the family environment. Other places like school, or places where you spent a lot of time, also played a role in shaping your inner child.

Write down all the memories and physical sensations that come to mind, no matter how fragmented they seem. Jot down the tones of voice, expressions, and words your parents or teachers used when interacting with you.

Don't dismiss any memory, no matter how silly or excessive it may seem to you now as an adult. It's crucial to acknowledge and honor the authentic experiences of your inner child, even if they seem absurd or exaggerated from an adult perspective.

The more detail and emotion you capture for each stage of childhood, the stronger the connection you'll make with that part of your inner self. And I'll guide you through the process of doing just that. This exercise can paint a vivid picture of the emotional journey the client experienced in their formative years.

When exploring past triggers, the Identifying Childhood Triggers worksheet can be useful in recognizing patterns of emotional response in the present. Work to identify one or more situations that have upset you and analyze the feelings, body sensations, and reactions that arise. Consider if the situation is a recurring issue and if it reminds you of any past experiences. By exploring and identifying these childhood triggers, you can take steps towards healing and move forward.

Exercise 6. Look In the Mirror

Mirror work is a self-reflection and self-affirmation practice that involves speaking positive statements to yourself while looking in the mirror. However, it's important to tailor the practice to your own needs and preferences.

Here are some fundamental principles of mirror work to keep in mind:

1. Use affirmations that resonate with you; affirmations help to counteract negative self-talk and reprogram the mind. They can be spontaneous or chosen from a list. For example, if you feel ugly, you can affirm to yourself by saying, "I have a beautiful heart and soul." If you feel uncomfortable, you can affirm, "It's okay to feel uncomfortable, I accept myself as I am."

2. Dedicate at least 2 minutes every day; mirror work is most effective when done consistently over time. Aim for a minimum of 2 minutes a day, with 10 minutes or more being ideal.

3. Do mirror work in private; choose a quiet, private place where you won't be disturbed, such as a bathroom cubicle or a room in your home.

4. It's okay to feel emotional; allow yourself to feel whatever comes up during the practice.

5. Keep a journal; record any notable experiences to reflect on your progress and growth.

To start your mirror work practice, follow these steps:

1. Commit yourself to regular practice.

2. Decide the best time of day for you. You can do mirror work in the morning, at night, or even during the day when you pass mirrors.

3. Choose or create your own affirmations. Make sure they are phrased positively and sincerely reflect how you feel.

4. Look in the mirror and speak the affirmations to yourself.

5. Repeat the practice daily and reflect on your experiences in your journal.

It's important to remember that mirror work is a personal practice, and everyone's experience will be different. The goal is to offer sincere love and positive affirmations to yourself, not to sugarcoat your feelings or be disingenuous. If an affirmation feels too difficult, start with a milder one and work your way up. The key is to find what works best for you and to be consistent in your practice.

Exercise 7. Be the Support You Always Needed

Nurturing your inner child can bring comfort and solace. Hold onto yourself tightly, whether rocking or simply sitting still and letting the tears flow. Dedicate just three minutes each day to this self-care practice.

Another technique that can help you process trauma is the Butterfly Hug. This exercise is used by trauma therapists in Eye Movement Desensitization and Reprogramming (EMDR) therapy. The steps are simple:

Cross your arms over your chest and join your thumbs together to form the butterfly's body. Place your fingertips just below your collarbone and alternate tapping your chest with each hand. While doing this, take slow, deep breaths and mindfully observe your thoughts and feelings without judgment.

You can also try guided meditations or visualization exercises to connect with your inner child. These can help you relax and focus on your inner feelings, allowing you to access parts of yourself that you may have forgotten. And, most importantly, don't be afraid to have fun! Inner children love to play, so let loose and be silly; it's not just for kids!

Exercise 8. Look Out for The Triggers

What sound, remark, or place makes your past memories come flooding back? What moments or things do you find yourself overreacting to? What are the things that bring out a big emotional response from you?

Why did you get so defensive when they complimented you? Or why did that child hugging his mother make the wind of jealousy swirl within you? Why did your dad's actions make you so angry?

Keep an eye out for these moments that make you emotional or trigger some kind of bad memories. Ask yourself:

1. Why does it make you feel that way?

2. What made you say that in response?

3. Why do you not like that saying or that act?

4. What does it make you feel?

5. What can you do to make yourself overcome the feeling?

6. How do you react to the situation?

Consider how your childhood experiences may be impacting your current relationships. Do you struggle to trust others, form close bonds, or communicate your needs and feelings? Are you prone to repeating patterns of behavior that keep you stuck in negative or unhealthy relationships? Are there areas where you may feel stuck, stagnant, or unfulfilled in your personal or professional life?

Exercise 9. What Really Happened?

You have things constantly running in your mind, memories invading your thought process and moments from the past that still haunt you and keep you up at night. While it may not sound appealing, revisiting that memory may help you heal from it. Find a quiet spot in your house and try visualizing the exact moment. Walk through the entire traumatic experience and start asking yourself questions.

1. What was happening at the time?

2. What were you feeling at the moment?

3. What were they feeling at the time?

4. Why do you carry the hurt of this time?

Once you view the moment from the point of your inner child, you might be kinder to yourself. Going back to the moment without trying to block it from your memory continuously and wishing things would have occurred otherwise will give you a certain closure.

Exercise 10. Positive Journal

From the name, you probably might think that this is something that hippie millennials do to seem Instagram-worthy, but it has many benefits. The intentions you set after waking up carry throughout your day. Your entire day will be bad if you wake up in a bad mindset. However, if you wake up with a mindset of being productive and getting things done, you will likely get more tasks checked off your to-do list.

Having a positive journal or gratitude journal does the same thing, but with your entire life, not just your day. It reminds you of the important things in life and pushes you to continue on the self-healing journey.

Take a little time every day and start thinking about your day. Ask yourself questions such as:

1. What made you smile today?

2. What are you grateful for today?

3. What is something that you are looking forward to today/tomorrow?

4. What sort of self-care did you do today?

5. What obstacles did you overcome today?

6. What things did you forgive yourself for?

7. What new things did you find out about yourself?

8. What mistakes did you make today that you learned from?

9. What do you love about yourself?

10. What made you appreciate yourself today?

Giving things a positive spin will help change the view of your day. Instead of being upset over how things took place, you will allow yourself to learn from them and move on healthily. It will also help you see the good side of life and love yourself on a deeper level.

Exercise 11. Go Back to The Happy Days

We have been so focused on the bad stuff that we completely overlooked that there were many happy times in our childhood. Times when everything was rainbows, sunshine, and cupcakes. Everyone has a safe place, a memory of visualization that makes you feel calm, protected, and happy. It is time that you find yours.

Go back to the days that make you smile like an idiot. Is it a memory of you fighting with your siblings or the elaborate prank you pulled on them? Is it your memory of baking with your grandmother while she feeds you raw cookie dough? Or when you went out for a picnic on the beach, and your dad made you laugh so much your belly started aching?

Thinking back to the time that made you feel cherished, complete, and safe will bring you a certain calmness. You can use this exact memory to calm your nerves when you feel overwhelmed or anxious. Try to sense how this certain recollection makes you feel and embrace it.

One thing to keep in mind is that reconnecting with your inner child is a process, and it may not always be easy. It's also important to have a therapy professional to guide you. But just like a lost toy, the more you look for it, the easier it is to find.

Remember, your inner child is a special and valuable part of yourself. Reconnecting with them can help you heal old wounds and lead a more fulfilling life.

Finding a balance in life can be challenging, but it's not impossible. When you're stuck and unable to move forward, it's important to remember that there is a middle ground where you can find your footing and overcome the obstacles in your way.

CHAPTER 8: WHY IS INNER-CHILD HEALING IMPORTANT?

Ignoring the wounds of our past can be a devastating mistake. If we were mistreated, neglected, or traumatized as children, our inner child carries the scars of those experiences. And if we don't attend to those wounds, we run the risk of living our lives in a constant state of pain. Our inner child becomes the voice that whispers in our ear, telling us that we're not good enough or worthy of love and happiness.

But there is hope! Inner-child work is the key to unlocking the cage in which our inner child has been trapped for far too long. It's a chance to confront the demons of our past, heal the wounds that have been festering for years, and reclaim the innocent joy and happiness that was taken from us.

We must remember that as children, we couldn't understand or process our experiences the way we do now as adults. And so, when we look back on our childhoods, we must do so with compassion and understanding. That little child within us deserves to be seen, heard, and validated.

The glorious truth is that you hold the power to reclaim the emotions you once buried deep within. There is no such thing as the past, only the present moment. Those repressed feelings still linger within you, yearning to be felt. They are already shaping you, influencing your actions, personality, reactiveness, and even your physical health and posture. To access these emotions, you must be still, listen to your inner voice, and feel.

Leave behind the distractions you use to avoid these feelings—overeating, binge-watching, social media, daydreams, explosive anger, and the false image you've created to dodge reality. If you so choose, you can incorporate meditation to still your mind and become a witness to its attempts to avoid these emotions.

The path to self-discovery is a journey that can last a lifetime. To embark on this journey, one must be willing to look within and examine their true self, unencumbered by ego, denial, or false pretenses. This introspection can take many forms, from journaling and hypnosis to meditation and yoga. By removing distractions and tuning to the inner self, one can begin to unravel the truth about who they are and what one stands for.

Take the process of building confidence, for example. Inner work can help someone develop a stronger sense of self-worth and confidence. Someone may start by practicing self-care, such as journaling or setting boundaries, but eventually, delve deeper into exploring their insecurities and fears. By facing these challenges head-on, they can better understand themselves and build a more resilient sense of self-confidence.

Take, for instance, someone struggling with anger. Inner work requires acknowledging the harm caused by outbursts and learning to control one's temper. By exploring the root causes of anger, such as childhood trauma or past experiences, one can heal and gain a new perspective, free from others' opinions.

When you listen and feel, the emotions will surge forward with a ferocity that feels as real as if they were happening right now. This time, instead of running away, confront them head-on and feel them completely. It will be a daunting challenge, but that's why you buried these emotions in the first place. You must push through and confront them. Do not hesitate to seek support from programs and processes designed specifically for this type of healing. This is how you heal your inner child. Clearing these suppressed emotions from your subconscious, what some refer to as "karma," is crucial to experiencing true freedom and a pivotal step toward enlightenment and awakening.

The goal of inner-child work is nothing short of a complete transformation. It's an opportunity to shed the pain and trauma of our past, reconnect with the parts of ourselves that were lost, and reclaim the life meant for us. It's a chance to break free from the chains of the past and soar into a future of unlimited potential, happiness, and fulfillment.

Why Do I Need This?

You've finally realized that your inner child is the most precious and fragile part of yourself, and it's up to you, and you alone, to protect and care for them. You are their only parent, rock, and source of comfort and support. They are innocent and pure and view you as a deity who can do no wrong. They trust in you completely, look up to you for guidance, and rely on you for stability. No matter what happens or what you say or do, your inner child will always love you with unwavering, unconditional love. Embracing your inner child means embracing love and positivity, the very essence of your soul.

The thought of your past mistreatment of your inner child is a heavy burden to bear. You recall all the times you've been harsh and unkind, calling them too talkative, introverted, different, too sensitive, shy, or not good at sports. The pain you've caused still haunts you, but your inner child still loves and believes in you despite it all. Their love is a testament to the resilience of the human spirit and the transformative power of love.

You are on a journey of self-discovery, a quest to uncover the mysteries of love and positivity. You understand that love has the power to heal all wounds, to transform darkness into light. Your inner child is the embodiment of love, the very core of your being. The Law of Polarity states that everything has an equal and opposite force, and love is on one end while hatred and indifference are on the other. To reach the sun, to bask in the light of positivity and love, we must leave behind the darkness and the negativity and embrace love with open arms. Your inner child holds the key to unlocking this love, this transformative force within you. All you have to do is break down the barriers, let go of the past, and embrace the love that has been waiting for you all along.

Inner-child healing is a therapeutic process aimed at addressing past emotional and psychological wounds that may impact an individual's present-day life. The major benefits of this type of healing, as I experienced myself, are:

Re-writing natural responses to stress:

Inner-child healing helps you to understand and change your automatic, unconscious responses to stressful or challenging situations. You can re-write these responses by healing your inner child and developing more positive and effective coping mechanisms.

Discovering forgotten experiences:

The process of inner-child healing can also bring to light forgotten experiences or memories from childhood that have been repressed or suppressed. These memories may profoundly impact your behavior, thoughts, and emotions; uncovering them is an important step toward healing.

Achieving wholeness:

All wounds need to be healed for an individual to achieve a sense of wholeness and well-being. Inner-child healing is an effective way to heal past wounds and move forward with greater peace and security.

Success, to me, is more than having a mansion and a beautiful family. It is a grand opera filled with emotional fortitude, inner peace, and spiritual fulfillment. It's not just about flashing lights, material wealth, and fame but a triumphant symphony of love, self-acceptance, and a strong connection to one's inner self. The leading role in this drama is played by a happy inner child overflowing with love and surrounded by meaningful relationships, guiding us through the storms of life with grace and resilience.

Contrary to the common misconception, success is not just for the intellectually privileged or those who have hit the jackpot. It's an inner triumph rooted in emotional mastery and a tranquil relationship with one's feelings. A serene inner child, unburdened by turmoil and chaos, holds the key to a life filled with success and fulfillment, no matter what obstacles may arise.

Finding a balance in life can be challenging, but it's not impossible. When you're stuck and unable to move forward, it's important to remember that there is a middle ground where you can find your footing and overcome the obstacles in your way.

To truly thrive, it's crucial to cultivate a delicate balance between creativity, flexibility, responsibility, connectivity, and consistency. This is where your adult self and inner child must come together, get to know one another, and form a collaborative partnership. Only then can you create a harmonious team where both your practical needs and playful desires are met.

Think of it as a journey of self-discovery and growth, where you can embrace your innermost desires and work towards fulfilling them responsibly and meaningfully.

Take that first step towards finding balance and watch as the pieces of your life come together seamlessly, creating a beautiful and fulfilling existence.

The Magic of Life

Why does your inner child shine so brightly? Every new experience and sensation is met with awe and wonder, fully absorbed in the present moment. Don't you long to return to those carefree days where life was full of pure joy and excitement?

Why not stay up way past your bedtime and bask in the mesmerizing glow of cartoons? Why not make a complete mess of your room for one day? Why not go back to the childhood video games that you so loved? Why not embrace the individuality and flair of mismatched socks?

But then, the cruel hands of society reach out, slowly choking the life out of your inner child. Beliefs are thrust upon you, taking away pieces of your creativity and innocence until you find yourself buried under the weight of societal norms and expectations. The once vibrant and imaginative child within you is suppressed, dulled by the monotony of adulthood. Stress and worry consume you, and you can't help but feel envious of the children who still believe in the magic of the world and all its possibilities.

But it's not too late. It's time to reclaim your unique personal reality and reignite the spark of your inner child. Embrace the thrill of new experiences and allow yourself to be fully present in the moment. Let go of the stress and worries and allow the joy and excitement to wash over you. Let's embark on a journey together to reconnect with your inner child and rediscover the beauty of life.

You, my friend, are unencumbered by the heavy burden of human knowledge, personal memories, and possibly even scars from the past. In this moment, you exist in a state of pure being, experiencing both the external and internal worlds with a child-like wonder, untainted by judgment or preconceived notions.

Your incredible memory and intellect have empowered you to navigate and control the physical world around you, leading to the progress and evolution of society. But the universe is a strange and ever-changing place where patterns emerge from chaos, but nothing is truly consistent.

Consider the changing leaves of autumn. Each one is unique in its shape, color, and pattern, yet we group them all under the umbrella of "fall foliage." This is just like how we categorize everything in our world, from people to places to things. We see the laws of nature and the objects before us as solid and unchanging, but in reality, they are mere constructs of our minds. We can imagine the perfect circle, but no object in nature will ever perfectly embody that form. Everything is constantly evolving, a dance of molecular motion that gives us the illusion of stability. This illusion is necessary for our social progress, but it also robs us of the magic of life and traps us in attachment to things outside of ourselves.

As we journey through life, the wonder of our youth slowly fades away, replaced by the beliefs and values handed down from our culture. We label and categorize everything, losing touch with the true nature of the world around us. We are passive observers, allowing the world to shape our perception instead of taking control and shaping it for ourselves. This is a dangerous trap, as we inherit the pain and suffering of generations past and carry it with us.

Bringing Back the Magic

The path to healing from childhood trauma is a journey of self-discovery that requires us to shower ourselves with understanding, compassion, and love. It is a journey that teenagers, young adults, and older adults alike can embark on, first in therapy and then as a daily practice. This intentional act of self-care and self-compassion is a powerful tool in supporting the inner child and begins with recognizing that we deserve it.

By becoming empathetic to the whispers of insecurity and fear within us and learning to give voice to the emotions of the inner child, we take steps toward true healing. We must treat ourselves with the same patience and understanding that we would offer to a dear friend, becoming our own loving, attentive listener.

As the inner child feels heard and loved, the qualities of childhood that once brought us joy begin to re-emerge. Playfulness, awe, curiosity, and the ability to find magic and beauty in the world are just a few of the gifts that come with this process. To nurture these qualities, we must consciously carve out space for them, setting aside time for creativity, play, and time in nature. Rather than viewing the world as a constant threat, we experience it as a place of wonder, magic, and boundless possibility.

Reclaiming our childlike wonder involves revisiting the parts of ourselves we may have lost as we grew up. Reflect on what brought you joy as a child and consider ways to bring that back into your life, whether through activities like biking, art, sports, or by embracing your spontaneous nature or playful sense of humor.

Help Is Just a Call Away

The process of inner-child therapy is a heart-wrenching and life-altering journey that has the power to heal our deepest wounds and transform us from the inside out. It is a two-fold path of self-discovery and growth that requires bravery, determination, and a willingness to confront the demons of our past.

In the present, we embark on a mission to rid ourselves of toxic thought patterns and replace them with healthier ways of thinking. We learn new skills to interact with others, build meaningful relationships, and connect with the world around us in a deeper, more fulfilling way. We delve into the depths of our soul to understand why we act and react the way we do, why we slip into our "inner child," and why we wear a mask to hide our true selves from the world.

But this journey is not for the faint of heart. We must also confront our past, unearthing the traumatic experiences that led us to retreat into our inner child. We must confront the beliefs we hold about ourselves, beliefs that tell us we are undeserving, unworthy, and that hiding behind a false mask is the only way to receive love and affection.

The therapy process requires us to break down the walls we have built around our hearts, shatter the false masks we have worn for so long, and learn to embrace the love, respect, and affection that we so desperately crave. And as we learn to do this, our inner child emerges from hiding, blending with our true selves and igniting a flame of self-esteem and confidence within us that feels nothing short of miraculous.

"Life is a fight. Don't let it overwhelm you. Adapt, and combat every situation it throws at you."

- Tim McIlrath

How To Know If You Are on The Right Path?

Healing is a transformative journey, breaking free from the shackles of the past. It's a feeling of lightness, as if a weight has been lifted off our shoulders, freeing us to reach new heights and unleash our full potential. No longer are we controlled by the events and people of our past, but instead, we hold the reins of our destiny in our own hands.

It's a euphoric liberation, a sweet release from the chains that once confined us.

Our inner child, once burdened by fear, guilt, and anger, finally emerges, strong and resilient. No longer do we cower in the face of adversity; instead, we stand tall and assert ourselves with confidence. We no longer feel ashamed of our experiences; instead, we embrace them and find peace in the knowledge that it wasn't our fault.

We let go of the guilt for the choices we had to make and find forgiveness for those who once caused us pain. We are no longer controlled by the opinions of others, speaking our truth with unwavering conviction. We break free from being a people-pleaser and dependent on others for validation, instead taking control of our lives and striving toward our goals and desires.

As we confront our pain and heal, we take the broken fragments of our past and mold them into a beautiful, fulfilling future. We are the architects of our own destiny, crafting a life filled with meaning and joy.

CONCLUSION

B y now, we have almost reached the end of this incredible journey, and I know you are ready to put this book away somewhere, perhaps on your bookshelf. But before you do, I would like you to read these final words of farewell carefully. I have written a little summary for you to make sure that the information we have shared in this book has fruitfully entered your mind. It would give me great pleasure (and be of great benefit to you) if from time to time you would go back and reread this part, or any other part, of this book.

Imagine being trapped in a prison of your own making, bound by the shackles of your past and haunted by the ghosts of emotional traumas. This, my friend, is the reality for so many of us who carry the weight of a wounded inner child, an innocent part of ourselves that has been shattered by the harsh realities of life.

"Darling, the world is not against you, the only thing against you is yourself."

Our inner child, a representation of our younger self, holds a significant influence on our emotions, behaviors, and overall sense of well-being. When it's content and at peace, we often feel a sense of calm and contentment in life. But when it acts out and causes turmoil within us, it can stand in the way of our personal growth and happiness.

Remember that these struggles are a call for attention from our inner child. It's crucial to give it the love and care it needs so that we can be our best selves and reach our full potential. Whether it's through therapy, self-reflection, or engaging in activities that bring us joy, taking care of our inner child can be a game-changer in our journey toward happiness and fulfillment.

Your Inner Child Is Calling Out

The fears and worries of our childhood linger within us all as human beings, but for some of us, the trauma runs so much deeper, silently tormenting our daily existence in ways that are often inscrutable. If you suspect the existence of a wounded inner child within you, there are certain signs that can shed light on the darkness within.

It is crucial to acknowledge that everyone can benefit from inner-child work, no matter the depth of the wounds they bear from their childhood. Though some may have deeper scars than others, the good news is that we all possess the power to heal and journey toward a brighter future.

Be Your Own Parent

The thought of becoming your own parent may seem absurd at first, but what if I told you that it is a crucial step toward emotional and behavioral healing? Say the words that heal. Say the words that the hurt child within you has been longing to hear:

"My dear, I cherish you."

"I am listening to your pain."

"You are complete and magnificent just as you are."

"What happened was not fair to you."

"It breaks my heart to think of the struggles you faced."

"I offer my heartfelt apologies for what you went through."

"You are brilliant and worthy."

"You did everything in your power at the time."

"You are the best."

Growing up can be tough for many people, with various challenges and difficulties that shape their experiences and personality. Unfortunately, many individuals are not even aware of the adverse events from their childhood that still affect them deeply, causing inner pain and struggles. This realization can be a heavy burden, especially when letting go of old defense mechanisms and roles formed in response to those past experiences. The idea of leaving behind familiar patterns and comfort zones can be overwhelming; for some, it might feel impossible to overcome.

However, for those who are brave enough to face their fears and strive for self-improvement, the journey can be both liberating and rewarding. Overcoming the painful upbringing requires a lot of self-reflection, introspection, and the courage to confront the past head-on. This process can be challenging and often requires the support of a therapist, loved one, or a support group. But those who persist in their self-discovery will eventually see the fruits of their hard work, leading to a newfound sense of happiness and fulfillment.

You Are All You Need

We often think that our inner self needs to be healed, but in reality, it's us who need the healing. Our inner self is already perfect, whole, and completely true to who we are. It's like the moon—it doesn't need to change or heal because it makes some people scared or causes tidal waves. The moon simply shines, just like our inner self simply lives its truth.

Are you searching for love? It's already within you, abundant and ready to be embraced. Seeking the truth? Your inner self holds all the answers. Need direction? Trust your inner self to guide you. Want a better understanding? Your inner self comprehends you better than anyone else. Craving comfort? Connect with your inner self and experience the unconditional love that's always been there.

We don't deserve this kind of love, but it's always given freely, like the air we breathe. It's not something that can be improved because it's already perfect.

It can be heartbreaking when we realize we've been neglecting our inner self. We may feel regret, shame, and remorse. But, just like the sun rises every day, our inner self will always be there, waiting for us with open arms. They never gave up hope or stopped loving us, even when we were too caught up in our own issues to see it. And for this reason, we would do anything and everything for our inner self. They are a part of us, after all.

This is the power of love.

It Is Not Your Fault

In response to the challenges faced during childhood, individuals may develop various psychological defense mechanisms and coping strategies to survive. These can take many different forms, depending on each individual's specific circumstances and experiences.

You may have lived through a childhood that left you feeling like you were not enough. Maybe you were taught that being "good" earned you love and praise from your parents. As a result, you may have internalized the belief that your worth was tied to being positive, productive, and helpful to others. But this sense of worth was not truly your own—it was based on the expectations set by those around you.

As you've grown and faced challenges, you've developed ways to cope with the world around you. But the pain of your childhood experiences is still deep within you. This held trauma influences every aspect of your life—from your professional and academic pursuits to your relationships with others.

If your parents didn't provide healthy boundaries for you as a child, you might find it difficult to set them in your adult relationships. This can impact your ability to form genuine connections with others and leave you with a lingering fear of abandonment. The result is a feeling that you haven't fully integrated all parts of yourself, which can hold you back from reaching your full potential.

It's important to recognize that these experiences and beliefs are part of you but don't define who you are.

Free The Shackles, Once and For All

Within each of us lies the power to heal, release our inner child from its suffering, and reclaim the joy, wonder, and creativity that is its birthright. By facing our demons, embracing our pain, and nurturing that inner child, we can break the chains of our past and reclaim control over our lives. We can heal the wounds holding us back, build self-esteem, deepen our relationships, and tap into the boundless potential of our creativity.

So, let me ask you: Are you ready to shatter the walls of your self-made prison, ignite your inner child's spark, and unleash your soul's full potential? The journey will be difficult, but the reward will be a life overflowing with wonder, joy, and boundless possibilities. The choice is yours; will you take the first step towards healing and reclaiming the life you were meant to live?

"Until you make the unconscious conscious, it will direct your life, and you will call it fate."

— C.G.Jung